FURNISH A
DOLL'S HOUSE

FURNISH A DOLL'S HOUSE

MICHAL MORSE

B.T. Batsford Ltd, London

I should like to thank all the craftsmen interviewed for this book, who have been most generous in sharing their expert knowledge so others can enjoy the same thrill of making miniatures. My thanks go also to all those whose work has been photographed, and everyone who has helped make this project possible.

First published 1994
Reprinted 1994, 1995

Published in paperback 1997

Typeset by Servis Filmsetting Ltd, Manchester

and printed in Hong Kong

Published by
B.T. Batsford
583 Fulham Road
London SW6 5BY

A CIP catalogue record for this book is available from the British Library

ISBN 0 7134 7878 0

CONTENTS

INTRODUCTION

This book is not intended to be an encyclopedia of how to furnish a complete doll's house (although it was tempting to try), but to introduce the average collector, of any age, to the various skills needed for making their own furnishings.

It is now possible to buy almost anything you need ready-made, either handmade or mass-produced (the latter usually cheaper and imported), but there is a greater sense of achievement in making something yourself, even if it just a blanket or a bread dough loaf.

The book starts out with simple projects such as bed linen and food, progressing to miniature carpentry before finishing with casting and firing china dolls, which involves some outlay on machinery. Each section has detailed and illustrated instructions for making one or more items, with ideas on how to adapt them and produce further designs. This book is designed as a companion to my previous book *Build a Doll's House* which contains instructions for making a simple four-room house which can be adapted to five different designs, a grand six-room house and a miniature shop.

When I opened my shop The Dolls House in 1971, the first of its kind in Great Britain, there was very little handmade furniture available, and mass-produced furniture was all in the scale of $\frac{3}{4}$ in = 1 ft (1:16). Collectors owned antique houses and furniture, children's houses were modern, hardboard and plastic, and their furniture mostly modern as well. Tantalizing catalogues from America, where the hobby caught on some years before, showed fine craftsmen's furniture, and simpler pieces made in Korea, all in the scale 1 in = 1 ft (1:12).

It was some years before British importers made the Korean furniture available here, but now there is a wide selection of well-designed furniture from Taiwan and China, and the work of skilled British craftsmen is on sale throughout the country in specialist shops and at fairs.

New work was often brought to my shop in Covent Garden, which has since moved to Northleach, Gloucestershire, but in the beginning I had to search for craftsmen to make $\frac{1}{12}$th scale furniture and accessories. One modeller was more accustomed to building 0-gauge railway carriages, while others were architects, woodworkers, housewives and school leavers. I encouraged them to make furniture in attractive antique styles, pieces I should like to live with myself, or did already own in full size. Having grown up among antiques, and sold them for a while in Portobello Road, I am familiar with their construction. Over the years I have picked up many useful tips, but when planning this book I decided to ask the advice of the experts, and spoke to specialists in each field, who have been very generous in sharing their knowledge. There is a brief introduction to each of them in the section on Contributing Craftsmen on pages 100 to 103.

Bear in mind that an exact $\frac{1}{12}$th replica may not always look correct – the wooden legs may look too frail, a pottery teapot too small. You will have to use your judgement, and sometimes make the pieces a little sturdier to give a better look.

You will find that colours should be a little muted when miniaturized, otherwise they become too intense and hard; in the same way, the colours in a landscape appear paler as they recede into the distance, but only a painter will notice.

Study books on furniture, fashion, china, for authentic designs, and research the period chosen for your doll's house. Remember it can contain 'antique' earlier pieces. A comfortable way of furnishing is to set it in the present day, and either copy your own furniture, or choose what you would like to own, with an interesting mixture of antique and modern.

Finally, I hope this book will extend the interest in this fascinating hobby by encouraging all members of the family to take part in furnishing a doll's house.

PART ONE

SOFT
FURNISHINGS

BED LINEN

SHEETS, MATTRESSES, BLANKETS AND PILLOWS

MATERIALS & EQUIPMENT

For the sheets
– fine lawn
– lace trim

For the pillows and mattress
– striped cotton
– wadding
– leather and hole punch, or tiny buttons

For the blankets
– fine wool or flannel
– blue felt tip pen
– blue or cream silk for blanket stitch
– sewing thread and needle
– scissors

Making the bed linen

Simple bedding is the easiest thing to make for the doll's house. Sheets are made of fine lawn, and a well-laundered handkerchief provides the softest material. The top edge of the sheet can be edged with lace or even drawn thread work.

Wool blankets can be cut from cream flannel; blanket stitch the top and bottom edges, and rule blue lines with a felt tip pen. You can crochet or knit blankets, but I do think cellular blankets are rather modern. If you really enjoy knitting, you can make a knitted patchwork quilt (one of my customers knitted hers on darning needles, though it is now possible to buy very fine knitting needles).

You can tuck the blankets round a piece of plastic foam (or even polystyrene) cut to fit the bed, but to make a traditional mattress you need a fine striped cotton, like shirt material. Cut two panels, with the stripes lengthways, to fit the bed, allowing $\frac{1}{4}$ in (6 mm) for the seam. Cut a $1\frac{1}{4}$ in (32 mm) strip across for the side panels, which will allow a height of $\frac{3}{4}$ in (18 mm), i.e. 9 in (225 mm) in real life. Sew the strip round one panel right sides together and joining at a corner. Curve the corners slightly. Join to the other panel, leaving one side open for the filling. It is easier to use something that is already flat rather than filling it with something like kapok: you could cut several layers of wadding to fit, or upholstery foam. A realistically firm mattress could be padded with layers of white felt.

When the mattress is filled, slip stitch the final seam. The buttoning can be made by knotting each 'button', or using small discs of leather or fabric, cut with a hole punch, or even very small buttons, which stop the thread being pulled through to the other side. Start at one end, with a couple of stitches through the mattress, before adding the 'stops' top and bottom. Then run the needle through to the next button, and continue zig-zagging through the mattress to the last one. Bring the thread out about 2 in (50 mm) away, and trim.

A bolster and pillows can be made from the same material – but unless you are going to leave unmade beds, they can be made up in white lawn.

For the bolster, cut two circles $1\frac{1}{4}$ in (32 mm) in diameter, plus a strip $2\frac{1}{2}$ in (65 mm) deep × finished width of the mattress plus $\frac{1}{2}$ in (12 mm) for the seams. Sew up the tube leaving a 1 in (25 mm) opening in the centre, and sew the circles to each end. Turn right side out, and stuff with wadding. Another method is to add a strip to each end and gather it with a drawstring.

The pillows can vary in size. Sew up three sides before turning right side out, stuff, and hem the last side.

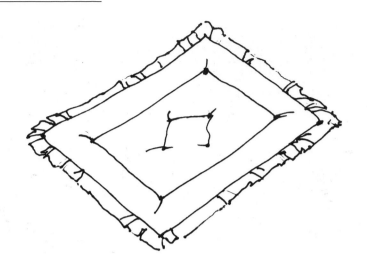

EIDERDOWN

MATERIALS & EQUIPMENT

- 2 panels of satin, watered silk or flowered cotton, $2\frac{3}{4}$ in (70 mm) × 4 in (100 mm) plus about $\frac{1}{4}$ in (6 mm) seam allowance on each side
- wadding
- sewing machine, with size 60 needle

Making the eiderdown

To make an eiderdown (*above*), cut the panels and sew right sides together, rounding the corners and leaving a short side open for turning. Turn right side out, insert a layer of wadding to fit, and quilt by machining a line about $\frac{3}{8}$ in (9 mm) from the edge and a diamond in the centre. You can add more pattern, but it will make the eiderdown very stiff.

If you want to add a frill to the edge, cut a 1 in (25 mm) strip, fold in half and gather; it must be machined in when the two panels are joined, in the same way that piping is sewn in to loose covers. As the frill will be inside at this stage, take care not to oversew when it is bunched at the corners.

PATCHWORK QUILT

MATERIALS & EQUIPMENT

- self-heal cutting mat
- rotary cutter and straight edge/ rule (for cutting a quantity of squares)
- scissors
- templates for hexagonal patches
- sewing machine, with size 60 needle
- size 10 hand sewing needle
- two contrasting fabrics, preferably fine cotton lawn $\frac{1}{4}$ yd (300 mm) of each, for log cabin, less for patches
- polyester thread to match lighter fabric, another to match darker fabric if used to back the quilt

Cut across and re-join one square along to form patchwork

Making the quilt

A patchwork quilt adds colour to a bedroom – even the Amish, who wear very sober colours, break out into bright reds for their quilts. A patchwork can be made of squares, triangles, hexagons or 'log cabin' strips – although this looks more complicated, it can be the easiest, and can be machine stitched. Quilt squares can be made by machining $\frac{3}{4}$ inch (18 mm) fabric strips of alternate light and dark fine cotton (*below*) together, cutting in $\frac{3}{4}$ in (18 mm) strips across, and moving every other strip one square down, before stitching together. This does require very

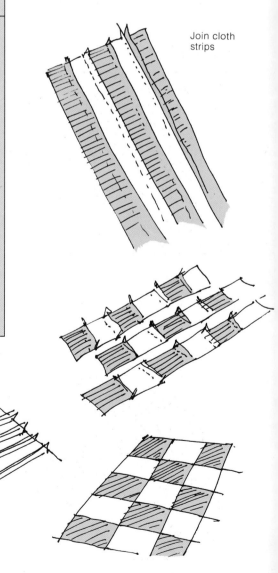

Join cloth strips

accurate stitching for the squares to match.

If you are cutting many squares, a rotary cutter, used on a 'self heal' cutting mat, is invaluable – you can cut several layers accurately along a plastic rule – the special ones marked in grids are most useful. If you can find architects' isometric graph paper (covered in triangles instead of squares) this can be cut into small hexagons (*below*). Some quilting specialists sell small metal templates to be traced on to paper.

Tack your fabric over the templates, allowing $\frac{1}{8}$ in (3 mm) turning, and overstitch together on the right side, using a fine thread used for lace making. There are not enough

Draw hexagons on isometric paper

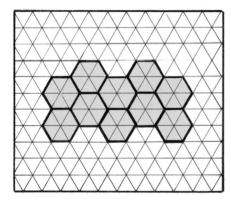

Cover templates and stitch together

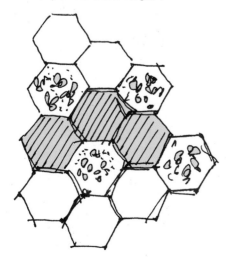

hexagons on a doll's house quilt to make an elaborate pattern, unless the patches are very small; try out your design with the tacked pieces, and chart it, so that the pattern is not lost while you are joining the hexagons.

Making a log cabin quilt

Log cabin is built up from two squares in the centre, with oblongs added in a clockwise direction (*right*), two light and two dark alternately. You can build up a batch of stitched squares by machining them all at the same stage. To make a quilt approximately 6 in (150 mm) square, which will fit between the head and footboard, and overlap the sides of a 4 in (100 mm) double or 3 in (75 mm) single bed, you need two contrasting fabrics – a light and a dark pattern, or one plain

and one patterned. The final size will vary, depending on the seam allowance.

Wash and iron the fabric, and when ironing, make sure the weave is straight and not pulled out of shape, because your stitching must keep parallel to the threads.

Cut two cardboard templates about 12 in (300 mm) long, one $\frac{3}{4}$ in (18 mm) wide, the other $\frac{5}{8}$ in (15 mm).

Build up in clockwise direction

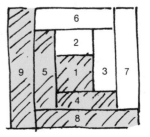

A panels

A panels

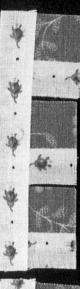

B panels

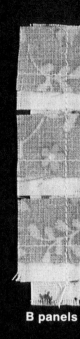

B panels

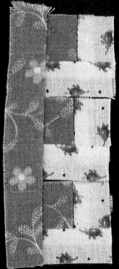

C panels

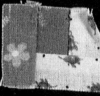

C panels

C panels

D panels

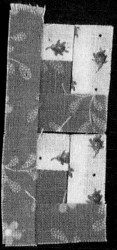

D panels

D panels

E panels

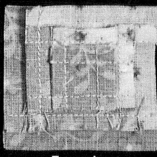

E panels

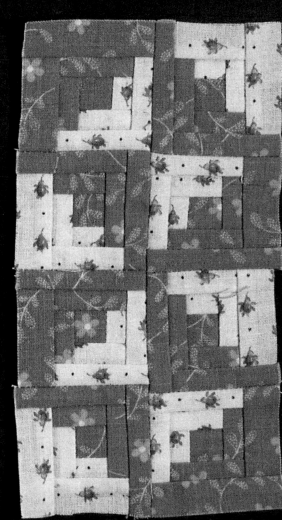

Finished blocks

Cut two strips of dark fabric, parallel with the selvedge, from the $\frac{3}{4}$ in (18 mm) template. Use the $\frac{5}{8}$ in (15 mm) template to cut nine strips of dark and eight light, also along the length of the fabric.

Sew a light strip to each $\frac{3}{4}$ in (18 mm) wide dark strip, right sides together, allowing a $\frac{3}{16}$ in (5 mm) seam and machine, using a short stitch. Press the seam under the light strip. Draw a pencil line across the right side every $\frac{3}{4}$ in (18 mm), and cut to make sixteen A panels. (For the following steps see the photograph on pages 14–15 showing panels A–E.)

Turn all the pieces wrong side up, with the seam to the bottom, and machine along a light strip. Press the seam under the light strip, and cut across the strip to separate the B panels: this should be at approximately 1 in (25 mm) intervals (the exact length depends on your seam allowance).

With the B panels wrong side up, the seams now left and bottom (the panel is turned clockwise for each seam), join them to a dark strip. Press the seam under the dark strip, and cut apart, again with 1 in (25 mm) spacing.

The C panels, turned with seams top, left and bottom, are laid on another dark strip. These should be cut apart at approximately $1\frac{1}{4}$ in (32 mm) intervals.

Now add two light strips, $1\frac{1}{4}$ in (32 mm) and $1\frac{1}{2}$ in (38 mm) long to each D panel, followed by two dark strips $1\frac{1}{2}$ in (38 mm) and $1\frac{3}{4}$ in (43 mm) long, cutting the strip and turning the panel each time. You will now be using up the remainder of the earlier strips, to make sixteen E panels. (The measurements of all panels are approximate, but give a guide to the proportions.)

Sew pairs of panels together, and press the seam open each time from now on. Join two pairs, to make a row

of four. Join two rows, then join to the other set of eight.

Check your pattern before joining the panels, and you will see that the squares can be all turned the same way, or light to light, although this can make too large a pattern for the size of quilt.

Cut the backing panel from one of the materials used, 8 in (200 mm) square. Pin wrong sides together, sew together by hand using a running stitch $\frac{3}{16}$ in (5 mm) from the edge of the patchwork. Trim back to $\frac{11}{16}$ in (17 mm) from the sewing line, fold over the front edge of the quilt, and hem, trimming and mitring the corners.

TABLE LINEN

A tablecloth can be made of fine lawn – simply cut down an old handkerchief (the embroidered oriental ones are ideal). Alternatively, you can use a lace glass mat, if you can find a square one, or a round one on a round table. Napkins can be cut from white ribbon, and rolled up to fit napkin rings.

Place mats can be made by tatting – a method of looping and knotting thread round the fingers of your left hand. An excellent introduction to this craft is given by Cathy Bryant in *Tatting* (see Publications). In tatting the size of the pattern is determined by the thickness of the thread, unlike crochet which is governed by the size of the crochet hook. If you are already a competent tatter, by using very fine thread instead of crochet cotton you can make some very delicate place mats.

The following instructions will make a place mat $\frac{3}{4}$ in (18 mm) in diameter. Worked on Guttermans silk thread, or Sylko sewing cotton, it takes 11 large and 11 small circles. Worked on Coats crochet cotton no. 100 or 120, it only

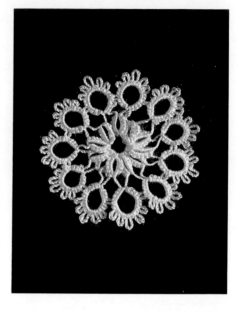

needs 10 large and 10 small to make the same size mat.

Tatted place mat

ABBREVIATIONS
cl = close
ds = double stitch
Lp = large picot
p = picot
prev. = previous
Sp = small picot

Use shuttle thread only throughout:

Small circle – 6ds, Lp (about $\frac{3}{8}$ in (9 mm)), 6d, cl;

Reverse work, leave a short length of thread;

Large circle – 4ds, Sp, 3ds, 5p separated by 2ds, 3ds, Sp, 4ds, cl;

Reverse work, leave a short length of thread;

Small circle – 6ds, join to Lp of prev. small circle, 6ds, cl;

Reverse work, leave a short length of thread;

Large circle – 4ds, join to last p of

prev. large circle, 3ds, 5p sep. by 2ds, 3ds, Sp, 4ds, cl;
Reverse work, leave a short length of thread;
Small circle – 6ds, join to large p of first small circle, 6ds, cl;

Continue until 11 small circles and 11 large circles have been completed, joining last p of last large circle to first p of first large circle.

Once you are used to working in this scale, you will think of many other pieces to make – antimacassars, crochet bedspreads, edging for pillows, etc.

CUSHIONS AND LOOSE COVERS

MATERIALS & EQUIPMENT

For the cushions
– wadding and fabric or braid, silk ribbon in 2 shades for 'patchwork', needle and thread

For loose covers
– fabric
– paper for pattern
– sharp scissors
– needle and thread

Making cushions and covers

Cushions can be made from plain fabrics, braid to resemble tapestry, needlepoint with a silk back, or interwoven ribbon to look like patchwork (*left*). Be careful not to make them 'oversize', although a real cushion 15 in (380 mm) square is not large, in $\frac{1}{12}$th scale up to 1 in (25 mm) seems big enough. Check the size and colour against your furniture before making up.

If you already make your own soft covers, you will have no problem re-covering miniature chairs. Cut a paper pattern first, pin the fabric in place, and glue or stitch together. Gather a $\frac{1}{2}$ in (12 mm) frill along the bottom to indicate a loose cover. Make matching piping by unravelling some threads and rolling them up between your fingers. Glue along the seams.

CARPETS

Doll's houses tend to have polished (varnished) floors, and loose rugs or carpets. However, a fitted carpet can be made from velvet, or some textured upholstery fabrics, while stair carpet can be made from velvet ribbon, or braid with a suitable design.

Even real stair carpet can be glued these days. To avoid permanent damage I have used wallpaper paste, but find that well kneaded Grip-Wax works best, and is ideal for keeping carpet fringes flat. Use fine brass rod for stair rods.

One solution for loose carpets and rugs might be to use fine petit point, which I found sold by the yard in Spain (it looked like old-fashioned bell-pull material), but it was difficult to cut the continuous pattern.

Alternatively, you can use photographs of carpets from magazines or the Jacquard-woven Turkish carpets made for doll's houses, both of which are very thin so the furniture does not tilt when half on and half off. I have used several lengths of the runners very successfully for stair carpet.

If you wish to make your own carpet in cross-stitch you can chart a pattern on graph paper; start with a simple Bath or Welcome mat. Some enthusiasts work on fine silk gauze, 100 strands to the inch (4 to the millimetre), and you can see their work at fairs and exhibitions, in the Thorne Rooms in America, or in the Carlisle Rooms in Nunnington.

NEEDLEPOINT PRAYER RUG

MATERIALS & EQUIPMENT

- 22 mesh mono canvas
- tapestry needle size 24
- 8 skeins of DMC or Anchor stranded cotton (see Terracotta or Carmine Rose Colourways)
- masking tape

or:
- 18 mesh canvas
- 8 skeins of Appleton crewel wool (see list of colours on page 25)

For stretching
- a piece of wood, larger than the canvas and at least $\frac{1}{2}$ in (12 mm) thick
- an old towel
- plenty of rustproof tacks
- a small hammer
- steel rule
- sponge

Making the prayer rug

This beautiful prayer rug is copied from a Kazak design which was woven by one of the nomadic tribes living in the region around Mount Ararat, the mountain on which Noah's Ark is reputed to have come to rest. It has a wine glass and leaf border which is typical.

Worked in crewel wool on 18 mesh canvas, it makes up $8\frac{3}{4} \times 4\frac{3}{4}$ in (220 × 120 mm), so allow at least 2 in (50 mm) all round; in stranded cotton it will be $7 \times 3\frac{7}{8}$ in (175 mm × 98 mm). Tape the edges, so that they will not scratch your hand.

You will need a tapestry needle, and eight skeins of stranded cotton chosen from the colour chart (pages 22–24) or crewel wool. A frame or picture bar stretchers are recommended for working the rug. If your frame is too big, sew strips of calico or similar fabric firmly to each edge of the canvas before mounting.

When using stranded cotton, the needle should be threaded with the end that comes off the skein first. Three individual threads (the strand has six) *only* should be used at one time; they should be stripped before threading. To strip the cotton, pull individual threads apart from the leading end and run your fingers down each one, put three back together and thread the needle. If you pull the stranded cotton from the wrong end it will go into knots.

Follow the chart (*overleaf*) carefully with the colours according to the Key. Start with the outer frame shown on the chart, work the 43 stitches in biscuit (alternate stitches) along the top of the rug and 80 down one side to give the overall dimension, then work progressively down the rug.

This chart indicates the Carmine Rose Colourway. Follow the colour keys for Terracotta
Colourway and Crewel Wool in Blue

Carmine Rose Colourway (Stranded Cotton on 22 mesh canvas)

DMC ref	Name	Anchor	Key
3024	Grey	397	
950	Cinnamon	368	
926	Tapestry Blue	850	
793	Delphinium	122	
3689	Lilac	103	
553	Violet	098	
917	Old Rose	078	
3685	Carmine Rose	045	

Terracotta Colourway

DMC ref	Name	Anchor	Key
–	Ecru	390	
738	Snuff Brown	373	
356	Terracotta	339	
433	Peat Brown	358	
927	Tapestry Blue	850	
926	Tapestry Deep Blue	851	
436	Snuff Brown	875	
355	Terracotta	341	

Blue Colourway (Crewel Wool on 18 mesh canvas)

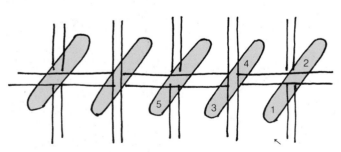

Key	Name
	Mid Blue 153
	Honeysuckle 693
	Mid Blue 152
	Mid Blue 155
	Dull Marine 326
	Mauve 605
	Flame 205
	Flame 208

The whole rug is worked in continental and basketweave (diagonal) tent stitch. Work continental where there is a single row of a colour, and basketweave where there is an area, however small (*see below*). If this is too complicated, work continental throughout.

Pick out the small areas of colour first, so that the long strands between each section will be covered when when the large areas are filled in. When you have to finish a thread, run it back about 1 in (25 mm), preferably through the same colour, before cutting short. When working basketweave it distorts the fine canvas less if the down line, when you have a vertical needle, is stitched over the vertical intersection of canvas threads.

All needlepoint is freshened by stretching, even if it has been stitched correctly with minimal distortion. Place an old towel on top of the board, and put the needlepoint on top of this, face up. Pin the canvas out with rustproof tacks, using a steel rule as a guide for straight edges. Pull the canvas gently so that the original size and shape is restored. Now damp the canvas – without rubbing, using a sponge. Leave

Continental tent stitch

Basketweave tent stitch

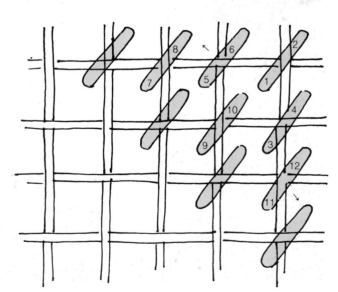

to dry naturally in a horizontal position for a day or two.

When making up, trim the canvas carefully to eight threads from the finished work. Turn the canvas over so that only one thread of canvas can be seen from the right side of the work. Line up the turned-under canvas behind it, and using a straight stitch, overcast the two threads, the one you can see from the front and the one directly behind it, all round the edge of the rug. On the corners you will have to make extra stitches into the same hole to cover the raw canvas. Note that the overcast stitches are *not* shown on the diagram. Turn the work and slip stitch the canvas to the back of the work, and back with fabric if required.

Prayer rugs do not need a fringe, but you can add one at each short end. You will need another skein of ecru, grey or mid-blue depending on your colour scheme.

Cut 5 in (125 mm) lengths of yarn, double them through the needle so you can pull the ends tight through the loop when stitched. Work from the back of the carpet, insert the needle two strands from the edge, coming out on the edge. Pull the ends tight through the loop (*below*). Repeat on alternate threads, and trim fringe to a uniform $\frac{1}{2}$ in (12 mm) long.

Carpet fringe

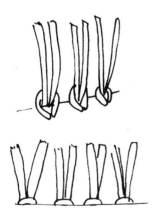

If you want to make a tufted carpet, you can use a loop stitch on a sewing machine, while a rag rug is made by pushing scraps of material through linen. A small hand loom can be used to weave rather ethnic-looking rugs.

ROPE KNOT MAT

MATERIALS & EQUIPMENT

- 6 ft (1.8 m) fine cotton string
- large tapestry needle
- 10 large sewing pins
- polystyrene food tray (or heavy card/scrapwood) to push the pins into

Making a rope mat

Make a rope mat to use in the kitchen in front of the sink. This was copied from a full-size rope mat, and can be made in fine cotton string, dipped in tea or coffee when finished to make the proper jute colour, or a skein of embroidery cotton of a suitable shade. It is woven round a pattern of pins, and after the first round the tapestry

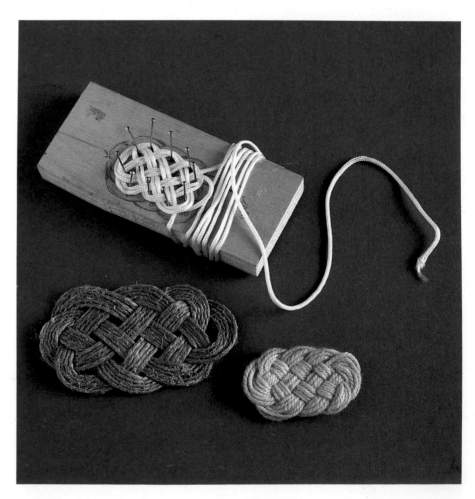

needle is needed to weave the string under and over the strands.

Draw the pattern (*Step 1*) on to the workbase, having worked out a grid using $\frac{1}{2}$ in (12 mm) diagonals. Insert the pins, to stand firmly where the dots are marked. There are eight rows of weaving (i.e. each one marks a change of direction). Thread the needle. You will have to work the whole 6 ft (1.8 m) round the pattern, using about 12 in (300 mm) per round, so choose a smooth string that will not knot.

Start with Row 1, and wind the string around the pins as indicated (*Step 2*), leaving a short tail taped to the workbase, to be tucked in when the mat is finished.

Continue Rows 3 and 4 (*Step 3*), 5 starts with a wide loop, to allow space for five or six strands inside the curve. Where Row 5 turns to Row 6, it passes under Row 1 (*Step 4*). Row 6 goes over Rows 3 and 4, Row 7 goes under 1, over 5, under 2 (*Step 5*), over 4 to become 8, which goes under 2, over 5, under 1, over 6, under 3. Make a large loop to allow space for a further five or six strands, as Row 5 at the opposite end, and start again next to Row 1 (*Step 6*).

Repeat the pattern keeping the second round exactly beside the first, the rounds must stay flat and not cross each other, or the pattern will be lost. Weave the second round, taking Row 1 over 6, under 3, over 8, under 4, over 7, under 5 (*Step 7*), and continue as before.

Repeat five or six rounds, until the mat is filled in. The two ends can be knotted underneath, or wound with cotton to prevent fraying, and tucked or stitched into the underside of the mat.

To stain white string, dip the mat in tea or coffee until the colour is correct.

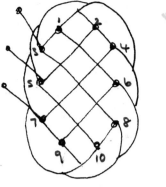

Step 1: Insert pins

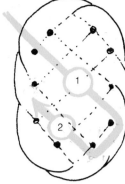

Step 2: Lay string round

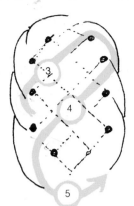

Step 3: Rows 3 & 4 over 1 & 2

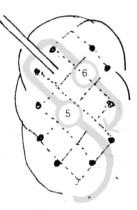

Step 4: Row 5 turns under 1

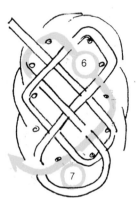

Step 5: Row 7

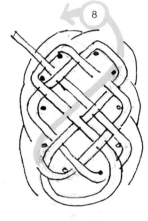

Step 6: Row 8

Step 7: Repeat pattern

PART TWO

CLOTHES

LINGERIE

MATERIALS & EQUIPMENT

- 10 × 12 in (255 × 300 mm) fine white cotton lawn
- 6 ft (1.8 m) of $\frac{1}{2}$ in (12 mm) wide or narrower cotton lace
- 3 ft (0.91 m) of $\frac{3}{32}$ in (2 mm) silk ribbon in white or pastel shade
- sewing machine/fine needle
- silk thread or sewing cotton
- a few $\frac{3}{32}$ in (2 mm) seed pearls or buttons
- fabric glue (optional)
- Fray Check
- paper for pattern
- small sharp scissors

General instructions

You can make a dainty negligee and nightdress, to drape across the bed or to hang in the wardrobe. These are designed for show, rather than dressing the dolls – the armholes will need to be enlarged to fit a doll.

Fine silk drapes well, while Tana lawn is easier to sew. Silk will need a double seam – sew right sides out to start with, trim close to the seam, turn and sew right sides together. You can use a sewing machine, with light tension, or handstitch with a fine needle.

Trace the pattern (page 32), which allows for $\frac{1}{4}$ in (6 mm) seams, and cut out the basic shape in paper. Fold the lawn in half lengthways, making it 12 × 5 in (300 mm × 125 mm) with the fold at the top. Pin your pattern on the left half, and cut out. Cut a curved neckline. Repeat the process with the remaining fabric, but this time the front section is cut down the centre to make the negligee.

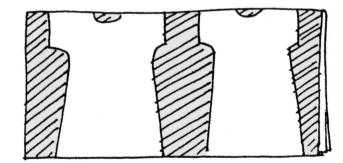

Fold fabric and cut two patterns

NIGHTDRESS

Cut 3 in (75 mm) of lace (you may need to trim the edge off a wider piece) and run a gathering thread along the straight edge. Draw this up to form a U-shape about $1\frac{1}{4}$ in (32 mm) long for the front of the

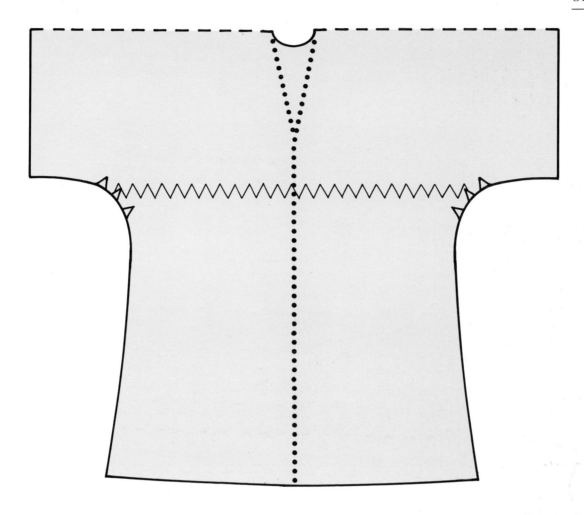

nightdress, and backstitch the end of the thread. Lay the nightdress fabric flat on a clean piece of white paper, and glue or stitch the lace in a U-shape on the centre front, leaving a space for the pearl buttons (*see below*). Gluing the lace is much quicker, and there is no need for hemming the edges of the garment, but this does mean it can never be washed.

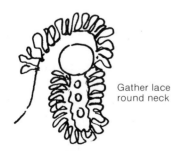

Gather lace round neck

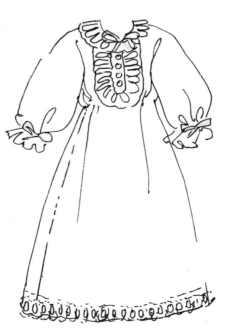

Draw up 4 in (100 mm) of lace for edging the neck, and glue or stitch in place, starting at the centre back where the join will not show, and finishing with a slight overlap. Make a tiny bow with silk ribbon and attach to the centre front of the lace collar. If you are stitching the lace, it must be added to the cuffs and hem at this stage, and can be machined. If you are worried about fraying, turn the edges up, not under, and catch them with the stitching of the lace. Alternatively, you can hem the raw edges by machine with a zig-zag stitch, and add the lace with a fine running stitch.

Turn the fabric right sides together to sew the side and underarm seams, and clip curves under the arms just short of the stitching, to ease the curves when the garment is turned right side out. Use a small amount of Fray Check to stop the cut edges from fraying. Leave to dry (about 10 minutes) before turning right side out.

Now glue the lace to the hem. Slip the garment on your left hand, like a glove, and run glue round the bottom edge. Press the lace in place gently without stretching it – you will need about $7\frac{1}{2}$ in (190 mm). Start at a seam, and finish with a slight overlap. Edge the sleeves with 3 in (75 mm) of lace each in the same way, using a finger to open the sleeve, joining the lace at the underarm seams.

When the glue is dry, run a gathering thread above the lace and draw in to make a puff sleeve. Make two more tiny bows and attach to the ends of the sleeves. A gathering thread can be added around the waist of the nightdress to make it slimmer, and to match the waist of the negligee.

NEGLIGEE

Lay the fabric flat as before, with the cut edges of the front $\frac{1}{2}$ in (12 mm) apart to allow for the addition of the lace. Starting up the edge of one side, glue or stitch round the neck (which may need a gathering thread to fit neatly) and down to the hem. The side seams should be sewn now, then the lace can be glued or stitched from one front edge round to the other, allowing a $\frac{1}{2}$ in (12 mm) turning at each end. Edge the sleeves as before, gather and add bows. Two more bows can be added to the bottom front corners as trim. Gather the waist, and draw in to about $1\frac{1}{4}$ in (32 mm) wide. Tie a 12 in (300 mm) ribbon in a bow round the waist, and catch it at the side seam with glue or a couple of stitches to keep it in place.

DRESS

General instructions

Study books on fashion – there are some very useful ones written as guides for theatrical costumes, such as the *The Visual History of Costume* (see Publications), with simple patterns of the basic shapes for each period, and tips on how to adapt them.

In general, try to use natural fibres, they are usually softer and drape better, and are more traditional. Fine cotton lace is difficult to find, but nylon can be used if not too stiff. Felt is useful for men's clothes, and for coats, as it can be glued easily (note that men's trousers were tubular with no centre crease until the late 19th century). Wool felt must be used for steaming hats (see Hats, page 38). If a colour is too bright, it can be muted by dipping the fabric in tea or coffee – the dress material illustrated was dipped in tea to make a more subtle pink.

MATERIALS & EQUIPMENT

- $\frac{1}{4}$ yd ($\frac{1}{4}$ m) or less of fine material for dresses
- white lawn for petticoats and pantaloons
- lace edging
- mother and daughter dolls
- mohair or viscose hair
- metal knitting needle (for steaming ringlets)
- fabric glue
- Fray Check
- paper for pattern
- needle and thread
- $\frac{3}{32}$ in (2 mm) ribbon for sash, neckline and hair

Making dresses

The dress patterns are based on designs of 1838 and make up into similar styles for a mother and daughter. The actual dolls can be cast from moulds (see page 93) or bought as kits, but the clothes can be fitted to any $\frac{1}{12}$th scale doll.

Make the underwear first, as the dress will be fitted over it, stitched and maybe glued in place (these clothes are not designed to be removed, as the sleeves are usually a problem).

Trace the patterns (pages 34 and 35), and cut left and right legs of the pantaloons from fine lawn, checking

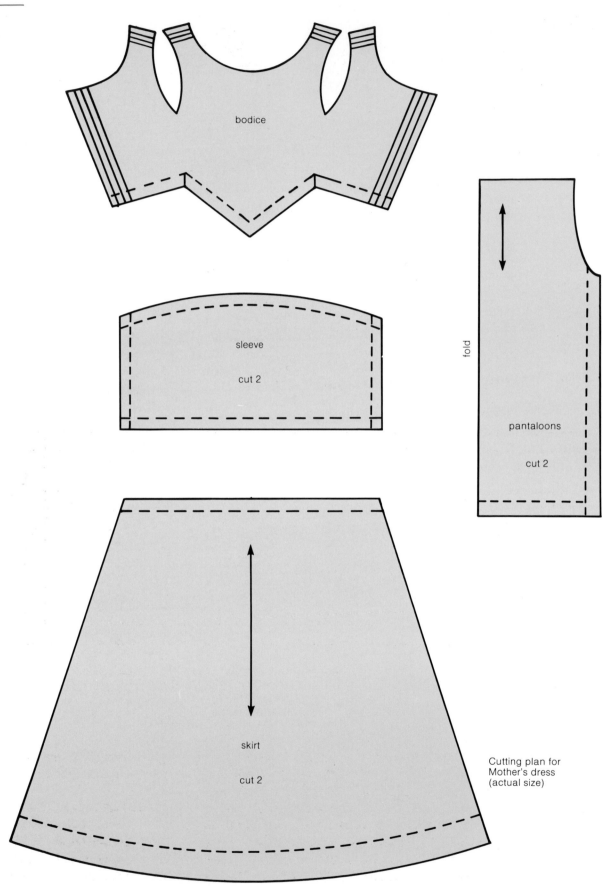

bodice

sleeve

cut 2

fold

pantaloons

cut 2

skirt

cut 2

Cutting plan for
Mother's dress
(actual size)

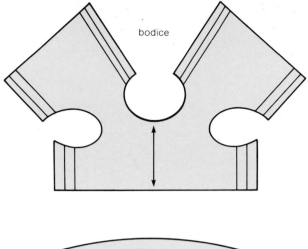

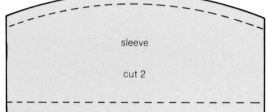

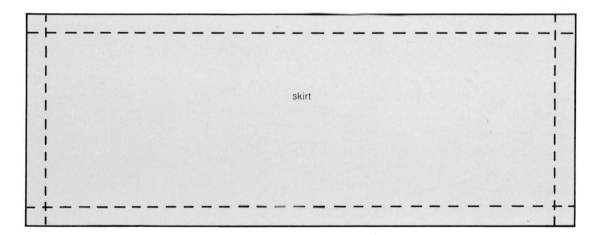

Cutting plan for girl's dress (actual size) – for pantaloons cut down those on page 34

the size against your doll. Turn the hems *forward* to the right side, and hold with a length of lace attached by a running thread and a line of zig-zag stitching. Sew the inside leg seam, with right sides together, and join left and right legs at curved seams. If the legs are too long, take a tuck in them (you will have to stitch by hand over your finger), and if too short, add more lace. Run a draw thread along the top, fit on the doll, and stitch in place.

The petticoat is a straight gathered strip the same length as the skirt and about 4 in (100 mm) wide. Turn the hem and add lace as before, then, with right sides together, sew the back seam, turn, gather the top and fit on the doll.

Use a fine cotton or silk for the dress. The pink cotton mixture used has a slight crinkle, and is very soft. Cut two skirts, and join the side seams. Oversew the edges, or spray with Fray

Check to prevent fraying. Check the length of the skirt, which should come just above the ankle, to allow a glimpse of the pantaloons. Hem or machine stitch the bottom edge. Add one or two layers of lace trim before drawing up the waist and fitting on the doll.

Cut out the bodice, fit on the doll, remove and sew the side seams, and neatly press the turn at the waist. The turn on the mother's dress must be snipped where indicated. Replace the bodice on the doll, oversew the shoulder seams, and join at the waist, either using an 'invisible' stitch – the needle goes straight up and straight down to make the tiny surface stitch, with a longer stitch below – or gluing lightly. Fit the mother's bodice carefully, with the point in the centre of the skirt, and overstitch the back seam. Then cut the sleeves and sew the underarm seam; draw up the top to fit the armhole and either sew from inside or oversew, drawing up the arm to fit. Attach lace round the cuff, and trim the neckline with lace and ribbon as illustrated, adding a ribbon sash.

Once the doll is dressed the hair can be added. The mother already has a moulded hair style, but is improved by 'real' hair – fine mohair or viscose fibre which is attached to the centre of the crown. This is brought forward to make a parting, then drawn back, covering the ears. A coil on the back disguises the bun, and a pretty ribbon and braid keeps it all in place.

The little girl's ringlets are formed on metal knitting needles, steamed to set them, then attached in bunches on either side of her face. The hair is turned under at the back, and a little 'coronet' of braid and ribbon covers her crown.

HATS

STRAW HAT

Making a straw hat

Plaited straw is available $\frac{1}{4}$ in (6 mm) wide. By drawing up the gathering thread on one side it can be shaped into a hat. You need about $7\frac{1}{2}$ in (190 mm) for the crown, $4\frac{1}{2}$ in (115 mm) for the inner brim, $5\frac{1}{2}$ in (140 mm) for the outer brim.

Start from the centre crown. Find the draw thread at each end, tease out with a needle if necessary, and pull up into a tight curve, taking care not to pull the thread out of the far end. Backstitch the centre in place, and wind the rest of the straw round to make a flat top to the hat; then butt join and oversew the two edges. Next, place on a shaped cork the size of the doll's head plus hair, and continue winding round the cork, stitching as you go. Tuck in the end of the straw at the bottom of the crown, and hold in place with white glue, to stop fraying.

Pull the draw threads at each end of the inner brim straw, and over-stitch to the base of the crown. Now the brim is flat, you can add the outer brim (*see below*).

Press with a steam iron or over a damp cloth. The brim can be curved up or down, and the straw can be varnished if you want a shiny finish. Trim with ribbon, feathers, fabric flowers, lace, beads (for miniature fruit), etc. Pure silk ribbon is softer to use than satin, which is rather stiff.

You can make the hat from one piece of straw, but may find it difficult to make an abrupt change of direction. A boater must certainly have three sections – a flat top, straight sides, flat brim – but a gently curved hat can be shaped by changing the tension.

FELT HATS

A variety of hats can be moulded from felt – the example illustrated is a bowler. Whatever the design, you need a good quality wool felt: if too thin, it will pull into holes, if man-made fibre, it will not stretch when damp.

Make a block the same size as the doll's head. Damp a small piece of black felt, and press it round the shaper block, which can be made of wood, cork, Fimo, etc., but should be protected by polythene or cling film to stop the cloth sticking. If you have shaped a mould for the brim as well, you may have no problem with it when you press the fabric in place. Stiffen the whole hat with spray starch, watered-down PVA glue, or wallpaper

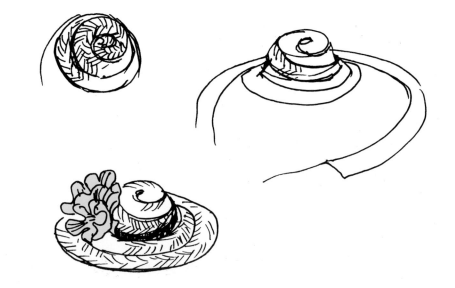

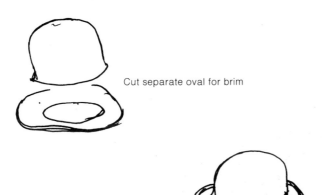

Cut separate oval for brim

Cover join with black ribbon

paste. The felt will keep in place when it dries, but the extra dressing makes a hard hat.

You may find it easier to cut a separate oval for the brim, covering the join with the crown with a fine black ribbon hat band, which can be glued over the stitching (*left*).

As the hat must be stiff, you can use any material – thin cotton stiffened with starch or sugar paste, papier mâché – strips of quilling paper could be built up with flour paste. As always, study the original to make your miniature the correct shape.

KNITWEAR

General instructions

Experienced knitters may be able to scale down some patterns to $\frac{1}{12}$th scale. Size 19 needles, set in wooden handles, and fine single strand wool are available from specialist suppliers, plus knitting patterns. For fine detail, use crochet cotton.

This pattern for a dress, bonnet and bootees has been designed to fit a baby $2\frac{1}{4}$ in (58 mm) long overall, illustrated in the doll making section on page 93. (Suppliers can be found in Appendices on page 99.) To fit a slightly bigger baby, use larger needles, size 14 or 16, which are available in wool shops.

KNITTED SET OF BABY CLOTHES

MATERIALS & EQUIPMENT

- 80 crochet cotton in white (Coats)
- pair size 19 needles
- fine white ribbon
- small bead or button

ABBREVIATIONS

k = knit
p = pearl
st, sts = stitch, stitches
sl = slip
st st = stocking stitch (one row k, one row p)
tog = together
rep = repeat
skpo = sl one st, k one st, pass the sl st over k st
wrn = wool round needle to make an extra stitch
wfd = wool forward to make an extra stitch
rem = remaining
beg = beginning
lh = left hand
rh = right hand

PATTERN

1st row: *k2, wfd, skpo, rep from * to end

2nd row: *p2, wrn, p2 tog, rep from * to end

Duess

For the front

Cast on 32 sts. K into backs of sts on 1st row to give firm edge

Work 2 rows in pattern 5 times (11 rows)

Work 30 rows in st st (41 rows)

Next row: k2, k2 tog, k2, k2 tog, (k1, k2 tog) 6 times, k2, k2 tog, k2 (23 sts).

Next row: k1, *wfd k2 tog, rep from * to end

Work 2 rows in st st beginning with k row

Begin armhole:

Cast off 2 sts at beg of next 2 rows

K2 tog at both ends of next row (17 sts)

Work further 8 rows in st st beg with p row

Next row: p5, cast off 7 sts, p5

Work 4 rows in st st on last set of 5 sts

Cast off & break cotton

Rejoin cotton to neck edge of 1st set of 5 sts

Work 4 rows in st st

Cast off

Back

Work exactly as for front until beg armhole

Cast off 2 sts at beg of next row, k next 8 sts, turn, cast on 3 sts for flapover (12 sts on needle), p to end

K2 tog at beg of next k row

Work further 9 rows in st st beg with p row

Next row: kp, wfd, k2 tog k1

Next row: sl 1, p to end

Cast off

Rejoin cotton to centre point of work, cast on 3 sts for underflap, k to end (15 sts)

Next row: Cast off 2 sts, p to end

Next row: k to last 2 sts, k2 tog (12 sts)

Work 11 rows in st st beg with p row

Cast off

Note that the whole of the skirt of the dress can be worked in a pattern as follows: instead of only working the pattern 5 times, continue in pattern for the whole of the 40 rows, omitting the st st. Then continue as for the other dress.

Join shoulder seams and neaten button flaps by attaching underflap inside and overflap outside at waist. Attach small button or bead to match buttonhole placing.

Sleeves (x 2)

With right side of work facing, pick up 20 sts beg with 1st of cast off sts for armhole, and spreading evenly along the edge to final cast off st for armhole

Work 2nd row of pattern once, then work both pattern rows twice (5 rows)

Next row: (k2, k2 tog) twice, k1, k2 tog, k1, (k2 tog, k2) twice (15 sts)

Cast off

With wrong side facing sew up side and sleeve seams

Turn right way out and press carefully, then thread length of ribbon through waist holes, leaving length to tie generous bow

If you feel the neck needs neatening, work a dc (double crochet) with a fine crochet hook. Alternatively a small overstitch is sufficient at the corners of the neck, or a fine piece of thin lace around the neck.

Bonnet

Cast on 24 sts. K into backs of sts on 1st row

Work 2 rows of pattern 10 times (21 rows)

K2 tog all along the row

Break cotton and draw up sts

With wrong side facing, oversew approx $\frac{1}{4}$ in (6 mm) seam from the crown

Fasten off cotton ends neatly

Attach ribbons at corners

Bootees (× 2)

Cast on 16 sts

K into backs of sts on 1st row

Work 2 rows of pattern 3 times (7 rows)

K12 sts, turn, p 8 sts, turn

On these central 8 sts work 4 rows in st st

Break cotton, leaving 8 sts on spare pin

Rejoin cotton to inside edge of 4 sts on rh needle, pick up 3 sts along instep, k 8 sts from central needle, pick up 3 sts along other instep, then k rem 4 sts (22 sts)

Work 2 rows in st st beg with p row

Cast off

With wrong side facing fasten off spare cottons neatly

Join underfoot seams and then back seams

Turn right way out, and pull into shape

PART THREE

AROUND THE HOUSE

TOYS

General instructions

Felt is very useful for making small toys, as it does not fray, but the seams cannot be turned. Pipecleaners are often used for making simple teddies, but those made from velvet or velveteen are much more realistic.

RAG DOLL

A rag doll can be treated as a simple silhouette, shaped like a gingerbread man, with a scrap of material gathered at the neck to make a dress (*below*), but as sewing the limbs and turning them inside-out would be very difficult, the side seams should be oversewn. Use felt for stuffing, cutting several layers for the body and head.

The following pattern is easy to make and uses felt, covered where necessary with white lawn. Pink felt can be used under the lawn to soften the stark white.

MATERIALS & EQUIPMENT

- pink or white felt, 2 in (50 mm) square for the body, arms and head
- black felt, 1 × 2 in (25 × 50 mm) for legs, or use body colour
- fine white cotton lawn, 2 in (50 mm) square for the hands and face
- wadding
- white sewing thread, fine needle size 10
- patterned lawn $3\frac{1}{2}$ × $2\frac{1}{2}$ in (90 × 65 mm), for sleeves, bodice and skirt
- matching thread
- matching $\frac{1}{8}$ in (3 mm) ribbon
- scrap of lace
- stranded embroidery silk for the hair
- blue or brown thread for the eyes
- pink thread for the mouth
- pink crayon for the cheeks
- sharp pointed embroidery scissors
- cocktail sticks for applying glue, and inserting stuffing
- fabric glue
- Fray Check
- tweezers or fine pliers

Making the rag doll

Cut the pieces out as shown in the pattern (page 45). Make the legs by applying glue on one side and rolling up into a sausage. Cut in half, checking that the length is still the same as given in the pattern. If you like you may attach a little lace or white lawn round the tops of the legs.

Make the arms in a similar way, then cover the hands with the small circles of lawn, fixing with a ring of glue round the wrist. Turn the sleeve fabric under approximately $\frac{1}{16}$ in (1.5 mm) at the wrist and shoulder and wrap round the arm, securing underneath with a fine line of glue. Lay the felt body on the wrong side of the bodice, fold the edges over and glue.

Fold the body in half where indicated, and starting at the shoulder sew on the arms and legs, securing the body as you go (*see below*). Hem the

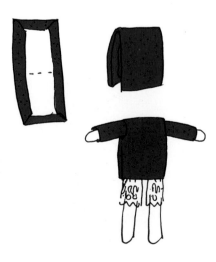

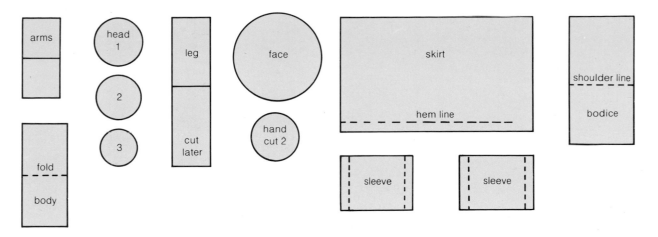

Rag doll pattern

skirt with glue and sew round the waist with tiny running stitches, then paint round the inside of the waist with glue and draw up the thread. Wrap round the waist, leaving the join at the back. Secure the thread and glue the back seam. Cut a little lace for the collar, fix this, and then tie a narrow ribbon round the waist.

Stitch the lawn circle for the head with tiny running stitches just inside the circumference. Lay the felt circles

on to this with the small circle sandwiched between the others, and draw up the thread. When a nice padded circle has been formed secure the thread. Sew the mouth at this stage and make the eyes with French knots. Use a dry crayon to 'rouge' the cheeks.

To make the hair, first cut eight lengths of stranded sewing silk (48 threads) approximately 2 in (50 mm) long. Laying these side-by-side over your forefinger, backstitch down the centre with matching silk. Brush the hair carefully with a toothbrush until it loses its clumps. After applying glue to the 'wrong' side of the parting, lay it over the back of the doll's head, starting at the forehead. Sew or glue into the style you want. For bunches, use a single matching thread knotted round. Finally, stitch the head to the body (*left*).

Once you have made the doll you can experiment with other designs, like the sailor girl illustrated (page 47).

TEDDY BEAR

Teddy bears were not invented until President Teddy Roosevelt's encounter with a bear cub in 1902 (although the Germans did make toy bears), and Shepherd's drawings of Winnie the

Pooh are familiar worldwide. The pattern on page 46 makes up into the typical bear, with a triangular head, seamed from ears to nose, a slight tummy, and jointed arms and legs (*bottom*, page 46). The overall height is 2 in (50 mm), if adding seam allowance, or $1\frac{1}{2}$ in (38 mm) if cut to the pattern size.

MATERIALS & EQUIPMENT

– brown cotton velvet, velveteen, or velvet ribbon 2 × 3 in (50 × 75 mm), or equivalent
– matching thread
– brown or black thread, for the nose and eyes
– scrap of thin leather or felt for the paws
– length of narrow ribbon
– tweezers or tiny pliers
– fabric glue
– wadding

Making the teddy bear

Trace the pattern and cut out the fabric with approximately $\frac{1}{16}$ in (1.5 mm) extra seam allowance all round (except the ears which will be described later). If necessary spray with Fray Check. Then draw round the

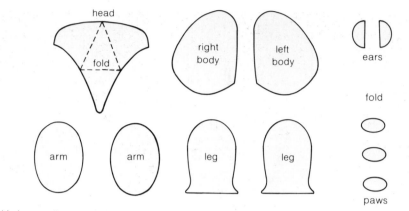

Teddy bear pattern

pattern pieces (on the wrong side) with a sharp pencil.

Paint glue round each pencil line, and work your way round each piece carefully folding over this line, checking that you end up with a shape the same as the original pattern. On the head you will need to cut away the extra material at the three corners.

Place the two halves of the body wrong sides together, and oversew down the front and almost all the way up the back. Stuff firmly and finish the seam. The neck can be finished with (one half of) a plastic snap fastener (to enable it to turn), or left open for the head seam.

Fold the head along the lines indicated and oversew (from the right side) along the nose seams and then under the chin. Stuff the head and either sew the corresponding snap fastener around the neck opening or sew the head on to the body. A bow round the neck will hide the join and also look attractive.

Make the nose and mouth with dark thread, and sew the eyes with French knots, or draw them with a roller-ball pen.

Make the ears with a piece of spare fabric approximately $1 \times \frac{1}{4}$ in (25 × 6 mm) cut on the bias. Spread glue over the underside and fold in half

lengthwise. Cut ears as shown, the straight edge being the folded one. Using the tweezers, glue the centre of the rounded edge of each ear to the top corners of the head. When they are fixed, gently curve each side round and secure with another dab of glue.

Fold the arms in half lengthwise and sew almost to the end. Stuff and then sew the opening up. Fold the legs in half lengthwise, and starting at the rounded end sew down to the bottom. Stuff, and then sew along the foot. Brush all the seams gently with a toothbrush. Cut three ovals from thin leather, two for the soles of the feet, and the other, cut in half, for the paws. Glue in place.

Finally, attach the limbs. If you sew both arms on at the same time and use the same holes on the body for the entry and exit of the needle, then the arms can be moved. Join the legs in the same way.

FELT RABBIT

Felt rabbits were popular in the 1940s. I was very attached to one with a felt carrot and boot button eyes, although I preferred the one in the shop to the one my mother made. This miniature rabbit can be made very simply by gluing the felt (*bottom*, page 48).

MATERIALS & EQUIPMENT

- grey or brown felt $1\frac{1}{2} \times 2$ in (38 mm × 50 mm) for the sides and ears
- white felt $1\frac{1}{2}$ in (38 mm) square for the tummy gusset and tail
- fabric glue
- (optional) scraps of orange and green felt for the carrot
- brown or black thread for the eyes and nose
- transparent thread for whiskers

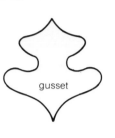
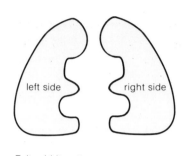
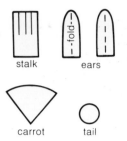

stalk   ears

carrot   tail

Felt rabbit pattern

Making the felt rabbit

Lay the pattern pieces (*above*) on the felt and cut carefully round each one. Using a cocktail stick, paint a thin line of fabric glue just inside the edge of the gusset, starting under the chin, and finishing under the leg. Press firmly on to one grey side piece. Repeat down the other side.

Glue round the head in the same way and continue until halfway down the back. Stuff the upper part carefully, using very small amounts at a time. To keep the paws firm push wire through once they are stuffed, or use pipecleaners. Stuff the lower part and glue the remaining seams. You will probably need to sew the junction where the gusset meets the back. Glue the tail on. Put a dab of glue at the base of the ears and fold in half; then fix by gluing on to the head. Make the eyes with single French knots, and oversew the nose.

To make the carrot, cut the green felt two or three times to make a fringe, and then glue the uncut part and roll up. Glue the centre of the orange felt and place the green felt on to it. Roll up carefully, and trim if necessary. Glue it to one paw.

Finally, close any gaps with a dab of glue and a little pressure on the edges.

WOODEN DOLL

A small wooden doll can be carved from a matchstick, with a sharp craft knife (*above*). Carve the neck and head, cut the stick short at $\frac{3}{4}$ in (18 mm), and split the legs like a clothes peg (clothes pin). Glue two $\frac{1}{4}$ in (6 mm) strips for the arms (if dressing the doll, add these last). Paint the hair black, and add dots for the eyes.

CHINA DOLL

You can buy 1 in (25 mm) china dolls, their legs and arms jointed with wire – some have painted hair, but acrylic hair can always be glued over it. Use very fine material for dressing these dolls, or knit or crochet tiny garments.

Tiny babies cast in one piece are known as Frozen Charlottes (after a vain young woman who froze solid riding in her sleigh without a cloak). The Victorians made cradles for them out of walnut shells, with a quarter cut away.

WOODEN BRICKS

These can be cut from $\frac{1}{4}$ in (6 mm) square strip wood, using a fine razor saw in a mitre block. Smooth the edges with fine sandpaper or glasspaper. The bricks can be coloured with wood stain or acrylic paints, and alphabet letters added from

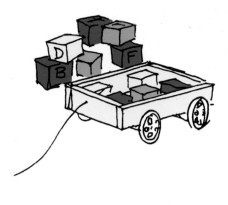

the rub-down sheets available from newsagents (smaller quantity and cheaper than art shop Letraset). Seal with acrylic varnish.

You can make a two-part box, or a pull-along open truck from $\frac{1}{16}$ in (1.5 mm) wood (*left*). Make the wheels from press studs, or cut thin slices of $\frac{1}{2}$ in (6 mm) dowel, then add a length of thread for the string.

There are many simple wooden toys you can make – an early rocking horse, a hobby horse, or even a doll's house (draw the windows, and make a fabric hinge or a sliding front (*see below*)).

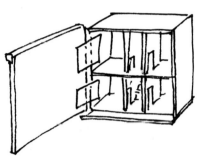

BOOKS

History

The Victorians used to print miniature books about $2\frac{1}{2}$ in (65 mm) tall, most of them improving texts for children, but there were some smaller ones for doll's houses, as well as magazines and sheet music.

Queen Mary's doll's house, built by Lutyens in 1927, has a complete library of contemporary authors' books, among them poems handwritten by Robert Graves, a mystery by Conan Doyle, excerpts from Rudyard Kipling, as well as sheaves of drawings, cartoons and engravings from Burne Jones, Russell Flint, Bateman, Paul Nash and many others, music scores, and even a contemporary copy of *The Times* newspaper.

For 'books by the yard' to fill library shelves, you can make mock spines on a block of wood; to indicate a set of leatherbound books, score and gild as described on page 53; a selection can be mocked-up by cutting coloured paper to various sizes to glue on the block.

Collectors

Collectors of miniature books tend to want them to be legible, and therefore over 2 in (50 mm) high and too large for doll's houses, but it is possible to buy some $\frac{1}{12}$th scale books and newspapers that can be read with the aid of a magnifying glass.

General instructions

For your own house, mass-produced sets of books currently available will fit most bookshelves, and individual volumes can be re-covered (see photograph on page 51), although the pages are not very secure, being perfect bound (cut sheets glued down the spine). You can make realistic book covers by cutting them out of advertisements and mounting them on blocks of card or wood; cut-outs from record sleeves can be backed with postcard.

You can cut your own books from any block of paper – a writing pad or notebook – to give you two straight edges. Hold firmly and cut to size with a craft or Stanley knife along a metal rule. To perfect bind the pages, coat the spine with a thin layer of PVA glue, first pushing the pad into a concave and then a convex curve before adding another layer. This will coat the sides of the pages a little and allow for opening.

If you want to make your own stitched book, start with a diary, visitors' book, accounts or autograph book. The pages can be 'bank' paper – thin typing paper used for carbon copies, or layout paper (spare sheets can be used as waste when gluing). Use coloured or decorated paper for the endpapers. The cover can be leather or cloth, or marbled paper. Full instructions on making your own books follow.

MATERIALS & EQUIPMENT

- self-heal cutting mat
- scalpel or craft knife
- steel rule
- set square
- bone folder
- 2 small boards for pressing
- weight
- needle and thread
- scissors
- small brushes for gluing and gilding
- 'bank' paper (thin typing paper) for pages
- coloured or decorative paper for end-papers
- leather, cotton or bookcloth for cover
- card for cover
- PVA glue
- starch paste
- Liquid Leaf metallic gold paint
- clean sheets of scrap paper

Making a book

Pages

Fold a sheet of A4 bank paper in half three times, each time creasing the fold sharply with a bone folder. Now, instead of folding, cut in half, using a steel rule and craft knife or scalpel. Fold each in half again, crease and sew through the centre, starting from inside the fold (*right*). Then tie the thread in

Stitch pages
starting from the centre

a firm knot. This is a section of sixteen pages – make as many more as the thickness of the book requires.

Trim each section at head, tail and foredge to the size you wish the book to be. Run a line of PVA glue along the folded edge of the top page of one section, place the next upon it and press well to stick down. Continue with further sections – four in all make a nice fat little book. Leave between pressing boards under a weight to dry.

Endpapers

Make a pair of endpapers by folding paper of your choice in half, and trimming to the exact size of the book block. Attach each endpaper to the book with a thin line of PVA glue at the fold. Press down well, using the bone folder, and leave until dry.

Soft cover

Cut a scrap of bias-binding or thin cotton fabric with the following measurements: the height of the book less $\frac{3}{16}$ in (5 mm) × the width of the spine plus $\frac{3}{8}$ in (9 mm) to overlap the front and back of the book. Rub some PVA glue into the spine of the stitched sections, glue the cloth, centre on the spine and stick down with the overlap attached to the endpapers. This operation strengthens the spine and endpapers when the cover is attached.

The cover should be a little larger than the book-block at head, tail and foredge to make 'squares'. To make a simple soft leather cover, $\frac{1}{16}$ in (1.5 mm) thick, make a template first by wrapping a strip of paper around the book-block and marking the correct size, allowing for a gentle curve over the spine. Use this template to cut the leather with a steel rule and scalpel, rounding the corners a little with scissors. To make a groove at the point at which the book cover is hinged to the spine, damp the leather with cotton wool or a sponge dipped in water and, using the edge of the bone folder, mark a line from head to tail. False bands can be marked across the spine in the same way.

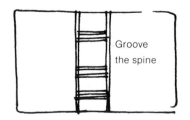

Groove the spine

Leave to dry thoroughly, before attaching the cover by gluing one endpaper, then place this on the leather leaving equal margins at head, tail, and foredge. Press down well. Now glue the other endpaper, turning the book to fit the remaining leather. Allow this to curve over the spine, and make sure the margin is even at head and tail. The foredge, if too wide, can be trimmed after the glue has dried. Press down well – do not be tempted to open the book at this stage as paper tears easily while damp. Finally, place between two pieces of clean board with a weight on top.

Remember to insert a clean piece of waste paper under the endpaper while gluing, to protect the book-block. Remove it before you position the endpaper on the cover.

Hard cover

For a hard cover, or 'casebinding', you need thin 'boards' which can be covered with very thin leather (pared even thinner on the overlaps), cloth, or a combination of both. Cut two small 'boards', using a card thickness in proportion with the book-block and the size of the book. Cut the card slightly higher than the book-block at head and tail to make 'squares', but the same width from the spine to the foredge. Now hold the two boards on the book-block, with an equal margin showing at head, tail and foredge. This moves the boards slightly away from the spine, and allows the book to open more easily.

Cut a paper template for the covering as before. When cutting the covering material, leave enough to turn over the boards all round. Cut a piece of paper the width of the spine and the height of the boards. Glue the cover material using starch paste for leather, PVA glue for cloth or paper. Then place the spine strip in the

Position boards and spine strip

centre making sure that it is well stuck. Lay the front and back boards in position, arranging them so that head, tail and foredge margins are equal, and leaving a little gap between the boards and spine-strip (*above*). Mitre the corners of cloth/leather, fold head and tail on to the boards, and smooth down well. Then repeat with the short edges. Turn over and run the edge of the bone folder against the edge of the board at the spine. Run the bone folder all round the top, bottom and front edges of the boards, and tap the corners gently to remove any sharpness. Leave to dry, then attach to the book-block using the same method as before.

Leather is easier to mould if slightly dampened before covering, but it is also more vulnerable to marks and scratches. The edges may need paring, to be thin enough to fold.

Re-covering a bible

You can re-cover a mass-produced bible. Start by gilding the edges of the pages. Hold the book firmly in its original cover. Brush on 'Liquid Leaf'

gold very sparingly to avoid paint seeping between the pages. Leave to dry thoroughly before removing the old cover. Make a new one using either method. The endpapers should be matt black.

Finishing

This is the term used by book binders for decorating and titling the book. This is a complicated process using brass letters and ornamental tools heated and impressed on gold leaf laid on glair. 'Blind' tooling is made with heated tools impressed on the leather without gold leaf – you can experiment making lines and patterns like blind tooling by marking the leather while damp. To make a cross on the bible cover you could also try using a scrap of gold braid or ribbon stuck down with PVA glue and pressed very well, or cut the cross from a self-adhesive gold label. You can complete a leather book by rubbing the cover with a little wax polish.

Bindings

A quarter binding has a leather/cloth spine and paper sides. Glue the boards

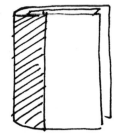

Quarter binding

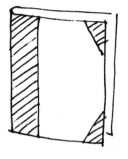

Half binding

on the spine material first, leaving it to dry and then add the paper sides.

A half binding has a leather/cloth spine and leather/cloth corners. It is made in the same way, putting boards on spine material first. Leave to dry, put on the corners, and allow to dry before putting on the paper sides.

A cloth cover looks good with a picture on the front cover – glue with PVA glue and press very well.

Headband

If a book is wide enough, you can finish the inside spine with a headband, glued to the back of the sections, in the space left by the curve of the spine. This braiding is made up with two contrasting colours of DMC or Coats crochet cotton. You can try out the pattern first with string, to see what you are doing.

Knot the two threads together. Hold in your left hand with the end between your third finger and thumb. Make a loop on your left index finger, and pull a loop of the other thread through with your right index finger. Pull the left loop tight, then make another loop of that thread, put it through the right loop, which is then pulled tight, and repeat until you have a length of knotted braid. Rub with PVA glue to prevent unravelling when cut to length.

Filling library shelves

An easy way to fill large bookcases is to glue a strip of leather on a block of wood, and score with a bone folder to resemble the spines of a matching set of volumes.

FOOD

Food makes a house seem more lived in – I remember Longleat, the Marquis of Bath's stately home, seemed more of a home than a museum, because the breakfast table was laid, complete with toast and cornflakes.

Antique doll's house food was cast in plaster – as Hunca Munca discovered in *The Tale of Two Bad Mice*. Now there is a demand for greater detail: individual apples have stalks, and bananas are realistically bruised.

The modelling clays that are hardened in the oven, Fimo or Sculpey, come in a variety of colours. Instead of using their exact shades, which make heavy, unappetizing food, buy a basic 'palette' of colours to mix yourself – red, blue, yellow, white, transparent – plus a few good pastry colours, terracotta and champagne (beige).

General instructions

The clay has to be well kneaded to make it workable, and becomes quite warm. If it is too sticky to work with, just leave for a few minutes, and it will harden as it cools.

Cut a piece of each basic colour you need to mix. Roll out into thin sausages, about 4 in (100 mm) long, twist together (*right*), fold in half, roll over, twist, fold and roll until the colours are thoroughly mixed.

Any alteration to the colour will mean the whole process is repeated to assimilate the new colours. If you prefer to use the clay for modelling only, you can paint the food with acrylic colours after it has been baked – which takes no more than 20 minutes at Gas Mark 2 (150° C, 300°

Twist two colours together

MATERIALS & EQUIPMENT

- oven-fired modelling clay (Fimo, Sculpey, or similar) in red, blue, yellow, beige, white, terracotta, transparent
- acrylic paints
- matt and gloss acrylic varnish
- glue (clear or fabric)
- linen for sacks
- $\frac{1}{16}$ in (1.5 mm) and $\frac{3}{32}$ in (2 mm) wood for chopping board and crates
- $\frac{3}{16}$ in (5 mm) square wood for triangular corners
- smooth work surface
- card, tin, pewter, china plates
- bowls, baking trays
- real food to copy!

F). The instructions on the packet tend to allow longer for larger models.

If using paint, you will not be able to make use of the transparent mixer, which is useful for the bone in a joint of meat, and blancmanges. Protect the paint with acrylic varnish – matt or gloss, depending on the finish needed.

The best way to match colour is to have the actual food in front of you – you can always eat it afterwards! Those who enjoy their food are most likely to make appetizing miniatures – you can feel quite hungry at the sight of mouth-watering roasts and cakes.

Make a note of how you mixed the colours, and if possible keep a sample of the clay or paint for future reference.

Making food

Fruit

Apples can be very hard to match in colour – they are really a very light green, and a good English Cox has vertical streaks of red. Tomatoes are also very difficult to match, and it is best to err towards the paler, slightly unripe tones of red. Oranges are textured by rolling over sandpaper while still soft.

Bananas look more realistic if ripe, with some brown spots. Grains of wheat can be used as dates, laid out in an open box, and you can make a removable lid with a suitably garish label.

Cabbages

These are often quite a light bluish green; to make very thin leaves you have to keep pulling the clay, and when it tears the ragged edge makes a fine edge to the leaf.

Carrots

Trimmed carrot stalks can be made from paper, the curly leaves from model railway moss.

Potatoes

These look best with a little soil round them. Roll them in Copydex or white glue, then shake them in a container with powdered soil from real potatoes – or if they come hygienically in plastic bags, use mushroom compost. When dry, rub the potatoes between your fingers to remove some of the excess soil. Make sacks from soft linen, which may need washing or boiling to remove the stiffness. Fill the sack with lumps of clay, and add potatoes where they will be seen (*right*).

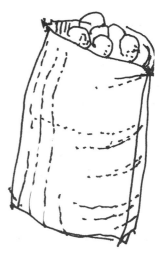

Cakes

Pastry or sponge cake can be very pale – mostly beige, with a little white; a dusting of icing sugar is white paint stippled on with a dry brush straight from the tube; a golden crust can be painted on with raw sienna. A good chocolate cake can be made from plain terracotta. For the cream, add terracotta to white (for a paler colour, always add the darker colour gradually to a larger quantity of the paler, to avoid wastage). Twist the cream decorations on a pin, add a twist of beige for the walnuts. A Swiss roll is rolled in the same way as a real cake – $\frac{1}{16}$ in (1.5 mm) of beige, a paper-thin layer of red, rolled to a $\frac{1}{4}$ in (6 mm) diameter, trimmed to $\frac{3}{4}$ in (18 mm) long with a sharp craft knife – take care not to flatten the roll where it is cut. Brown the sponge with a little raw sienna, stippled as before.

Fruit pies

Tiny coloured glass beads can be used as cherries or gooseberries in cut pies; plastic will melt in the oven but can be added after the pastry has been baked 'blind'.

Sweets

Look out for labels such as the small logo on the end of a Kit Kat bar: for a miniature Kit Kat, cover a block of card in the silver foil, and wrap round the small label. Tiny licorice allsorts are made by rolling out several layers of Fimo together (*above*).

Stilton

The blue veins in a Stilton are added after the cheese base has been mixed, and run right through.

Bread

A coarser grained clay, Das Pronto, makes good bread. Cut some thin slices to make toast, checking first that they fit your toast rack. A very traditional medium is bread dough –

equal quantities of plain flour and salt, mixed with enough water to make a firm dough. This is ideal for bread – cottage loaves, croissants, plaits, etc. –

and is baked in a moderate oven at Mark 4 (180° C, 350° F) over half an hour. Any other foods can be painted with acrylic paints, if not watered down. Even the loaves will need a little browning – rub some burnt sienna on to the crust with your finger. The only drawback of bread dough is that it will disintegrate in the damp – condensation from a window will make a loaf swell to a soggy mess twice its original size.

Strings of onions

These can be made with raffia – the only problem is making the clay onions stick to the raffia!

Strings of sausages

String these on to cotton, with a knot at each end – you need a very thin needle, and chippolatas are out!

BASKETS

MAKING A SIMPLE BASKET

If you want to make a simple basket, to hold eggs, rolls, or flowers, plait three strands of raffia, and then stitch the plait into a bowl shape.

To weave a proper cane basket, you will need fine cane, size 00, and slightly thicker size 0, for the 'stakes' or ribs of the basket.

SHOPPING BASKET

MATERIALS & EQUIPMENT

- 6 size 0 cane stakes 9 in (225 mm) long
- 1 length size 00 weaving cane
- 4 in (100 mm) size 3 handle cane (optional)
- bowl of warm water for soaking cane

Making a shopping basket

Cut six stakes 9 in (225 mm) long. Soak for a few minutes in warm water with a coiled strand of 00, until the cane becomes pliable. If the cane dries out while you are working, and makes sharp instead of curved bends, soak it again.

Lay three stakes over the other three at right angles (*above right*). Loop the centre of the 00 strand of cane over one side of the cross (*right*), and

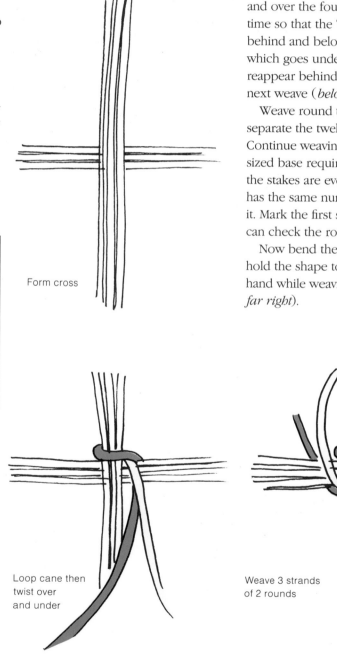

Form cross

Loop cane then twist over and under

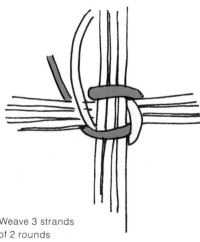

Weave 3 strands of 2 rounds

weave the two ends alternately under and over the four bars, twisting each time so that the 'over' comes from behind and below the previous strand, which goes under the next bar, to reappear behind and below for the next weave (*below*).

Weave round three times, then separate the twelve stakes (page 59). Continue weaving until you have the sized base required, making sure that the stakes are evenly spaced, and each has the same number of strands over it. Mark the first stake at the top so you can check the rounds of weaving.

Now bend the stakes upwards, and hold the shape together with your left hand while weaving the cane (page 59, *far right*).

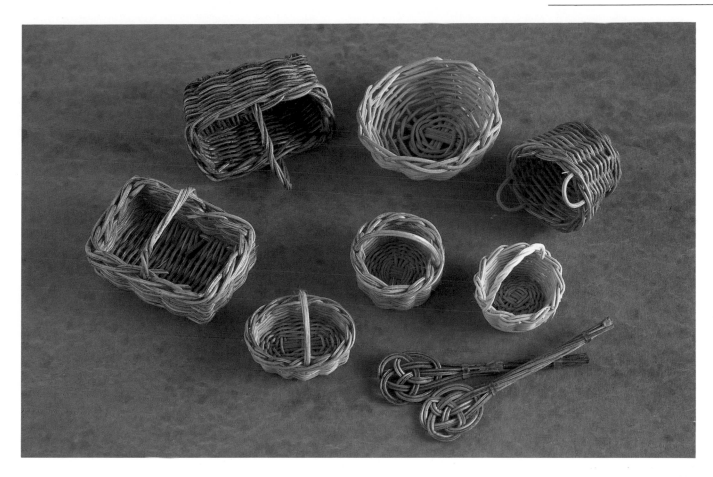

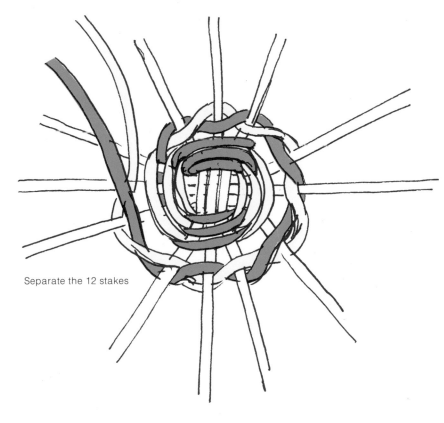

Separate the 12 stakes

Bend stakes upwards

When the basket is the correct height make sure the top is level, and the last round of weaving finishes at the first stake. Leave $1\frac{1}{2}$ in (38 mm) spare 00 cane, pointing inwards, to be trimmed later.

If you have to join a weaving strand halfway through, make sure you do not have to join both at the same place, and cut one shorter. Leave $1\frac{1}{2}$ in (38 mm) of the old and the new piece,

Finish top of basket

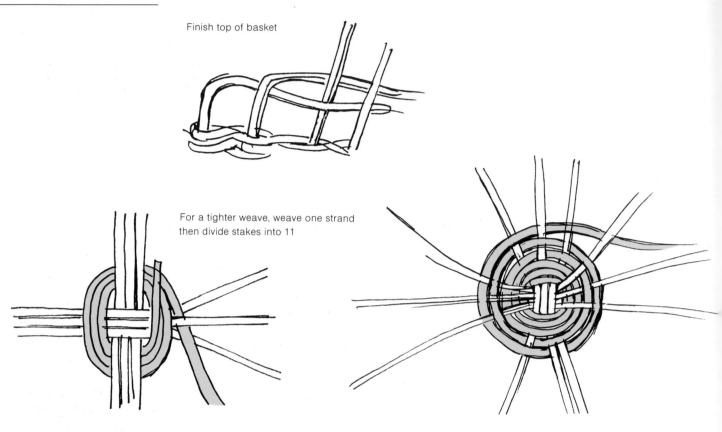

For a tighter weave, weave one strand then divide stakes into 11

to be trimmed inside when finished, and continue weaving with the new piece.

To finish the top of the basket the stakes must be woven in and out of each other. Bend one behind the next one, in front of a second, behind a third (*top*). Continue round the top until all the stakes are tucked down, and trim off the ends inside the basket.

To make a handle, cut two 4 in (100 mm) lengths of 00 cane. Push the ends down the side of a stake (open a gap with a small screwdriver or bradawl). Twist together until you have a handle length, and cut short, leaving enough straight cane to push down the opposite side of the basket. A single length of size 3 cane can be used for a straight handle.

For a tighter weave, you can use one instead of two strands (*above*). Keep two stakes together when dividing, and trim one off after two rounds, to leave eleven stakes.

Crates

Wooden crates for oranges or other fruit can be made from thin strip wood. The shallow boxes should have triangular sections (cut from $\frac{3}{16}$ in (5 mm) square) in the corners, and peaches should be bedded in blue tissue paper. The 'bloom' is added by rolling in talcum powder before baking.

Coal

As model railway enthusiasts have discovered, coal broken up still looks

like coal (*below*) – use it in sacks, or a fire grate – and small twigs make good logs. Make the fire glow with shiny red toffee paper or red sequins.

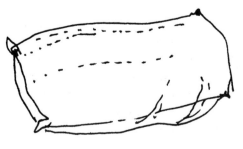

FLOWERS

MATERIALS & EQUIPMENT

- dried flowers, beads, vases, pots
- model railway moss foliage
- oven-fired moulding clay such as Fimo
- quilling paper
- quilling tool
- sharp scissors
- craft knife
- self-heal workmat
- clear glue
- stamens (for full size flowers) or fine fuse wire
- florists' tape
- coloured tissues, or tissue paper

Choice of materials

Victorian doll's house plants were often made of fabric, standing in turned wooden plant pots. Stylised cast metal 'flats' of an intricate plant in a vase were made in Germany, and there were realistic ones made of coiled brass sheet and cast Viennese bronze.

Small dried flowers can be arranged in vases – you can even grow and dry your own, while miniature rose buds look particularly effective among a few everlasting flowers.

The rubbery moss available from model railway shops, for hedging, makes good doll's house foliage, and small plants such as camomile and lichens can be grown sucessfully in $\frac{1}{12}$th scale unglazed plant pots. Air

plants can survive on the humidity in the air.

Fimo is a useful medium, but you must mix the colours carefully (see advice on food, page 54). To make thin petals or leaves, you must pull the well-kneaded clay as long as it will stretch. You can sculpt into a ball to make a geranium head. Anyone used to working in icing sugar will find the same techniques can be used for making miniature flowers.

You may prefer working with paper, which is already the right thickness. Quilling paper is handy, and you can buy a mixed set of colours which will give you enough for yellow daffodils, pink roses, red poppies, green leaves, blue cornflowers – plenty to experiment with.

Stalks

A bunch of stamens, used for full size silk flowers, will make useful stalks. You can cover them with green florists' tape, a thin waxy material, which can also be stretched and crinkled to make realistic house plants. To cover the wire, run glue down the centre of the tape, lay the stamen over it, and twist the tape in opposite directions, just like opening a toffee paper! With a bit of judicious pulling and flattening, you should have a thin stem. Leave a little spare green tape at one end to form the base of the flower, to be glued to the back of the petals.

Daffodil

A daffodil is easy to make, with three $\frac{1}{2}$ in (12 mm) lengths of $\frac{1}{8}$ in (3 mm) yellow quilling paper, cut to a propellor shape, to make the centre less bulky, and laid across each other (*below*). Use a clear, quick-drying glue (Bostik is recommended). The trumpet is made by rolling (or 'quilling') a $\frac{1}{2}$ in (12 mm) strip (*below*). Use a quilling tool, or darning needle with its eye snipped open and the point glued into a small length of $\frac{1}{4}$ in

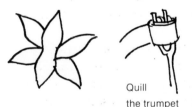

Quill the trumpet

down with a small screwdriver or similar tool. For the leaves, which are wider than a daffodil's, fold the paper in half lengthways, open out again $\frac{1}{2}$ in (12 mm) from the base, leaving a centre crease, and trim to a point. One or two leaves should wrap around the bottom of the stalk.

With a black centre, and more open petals, the flower can be a poppy. Remember to add a green knob to the back of the petals, and make ragged leaves. A fuller flower can be a peony, a ranunculus, or a rose – this has no coloured centre, and the petals can be pushed into shape, but not ragged.

Daisy

By making straight cuts along a strip (*below*) you can make a very versatile daisy, and vary the tone by using two colours, about 1 in (25 mm) for the centre, $2\frac{1}{4}$ in (58 mm) for the main colour (*bottom*). Pink and white will make a daisy, orange and red a marigold, shades of blue, purple, pink or white a cornflower. (Using a craft knife on a self-heal mat you can easily make parallel cuts, but if you use scissors you will probably cut off more petals than you make.)

Quill the paper, gluing the second colour at the join. Dab a spot of glue to the base of the flower to keep it together, then add a stalk and arrange tight bunches of flowers in vases or bowls, with a few green leaves.

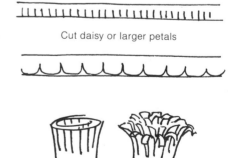

Cut daisy or larger petals

(6 mm) dowel. Glue the roll of paper to the centre of the petals. Before attaching the stalk, remember to bend it in a right angle (*above*), about $\frac{1}{8}$ in (3 mm) from the flower, to make the characteristic shape. As when making food, it is important to study the original. The petals should not be too

even (which was why I said it was easy), and some should be bent forward slightly. You can cut leaves from half the width of quilling paper; make a curve in the end by pulling your nail along from top to bottom.

Tulip

These can be made in the same way, with squarer petals, but are better quilled. Snip petal shapes in a $\frac{3}{4}$ in (18 mm) strip of red or yellow paper. If you work on a self-heal rubber work mat with a sharp craft knife, any cutting is much quicker.

Prepare a stamen stalk, but leave the coloured stamen free, so that you can roll the petals round it. A tulip will need a yellow stamen, and not many petals. Keep these straight, but make the tips lightly crinkled by pressing

Rose

You can also make a rose by folding the paper while quilling (see diagrams to the right). Start with three tight coils, and glue; then fold the paper down, parallel with the quiller. Continue to wind the paper away from you, allowing the crease to pull away from the quiller, until the paper is at right angles again. Fold down as before, and repeat until your rose is large enough.

Glue from the back. If you are making cut roses for a bowl or basket, just add one or two pointed leaves to the back. If you need a stem, cover the join with several diamond-shaped strips of green paper. Leaves grow in groups of three or five on a stem.

Another method, using any paper, is to cut the petals from a circle to avoid overlapping in the centre. Pink tissues (which are usually two-ply), cut into two different sized circles, and trimmed to petal shapes round the edges (*below right*), are glued then bunched to make a rose. Several layers cut and snipped will make carnations.

Tissue paper coloured with acrylic paint is very crisp and quite firm, allowing a skilled craftsman to make the most realistic flowers. The daffodils on page 61 even have the fine sheath that covered the bud, on a fine stalk of fuse wire, covered in tissue and painted. The paper is painted before cutting the leaves and petals, and glued with a spot of white PVA glue applied with a pin.

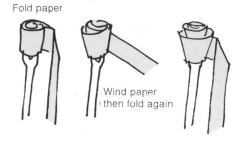

Fold paper

Wind paper then fold again

Tissue rose

Quilled rose

Petal cut from tissue

PART FOUR

FURNITURE AND PICTURES

FURNITURE

SIMPLE FURNITURE

Some doll's house furniture can be made from domestic materials around the house – matchboxes can be made into a chest of drawers, cardboard round a cotton reel base can be covered to look like a tub chair, and a divan bed can be made from a cardboard box, hidden under pretty bed covers and a padded headboard.

Wooden furniture can be made from sheet and strip wood available from hobby and doll's house shops: obeche is a firm wood, and can be stained; spruce has streaks, like a miniature pitch pine; while balsa is not recommended for serious doll's house furniture, as it is very fragile.

LADDERBACK CHAIR

MATERIALS & EQUIPMENT

- $\frac{3}{16}$ in (5 mm) birch dowel
- $\frac{1}{16}$ in (1.5 mm) birch dowel
- $\frac{1}{16} \times \frac{3}{16}$ in (1.5 × 5 mm) strip
- $\frac{1}{16} \times \frac{3}{8}$ in (1.5 × 9 mm) strip
- twine, or embroidery cotton for rush seat
- darning needle
- electric minidrill or pin vice and $\frac{1}{16}$ in (1.5 mm) bit
- vice (optional)
- PVA glue
- mitre block and razor saw
- fretsaw, or craft knife

Making the chair

To make a ladderback kitchen chair (a popular 18th century style), you need $\frac{3}{16}$ in (5 mm) birch dowel for the uprights, $\frac{1}{16} \times \frac{3}{16}$ in (1.5 × 5 mm) strip obeche for the back, and $\frac{1}{16}$ in (1.5 mm) dowel for the bars. The 'ladder' can be butt-joined after the seat bars are inserted (these joints must be firm, to withstand the pressure of weaving the rush seat).

Cut two lengths of $\frac{3}{16}$ in (5 mm) dowel, 4 in (100 mm) long for the back, and two $1\frac{5}{8}$ in (42 mm) long for the front legs. Mark the legs for drilling $1\frac{7}{16}$ in (37 mm) and $\frac{11}{16}$ in (17 mm) from the bottom. The tops must be rounded – you can rub down with sandpaper, or turn on a lathe (see page 72) before cutting to length.

The dowel can be held in a vice for drilling, or can be held firmly between two strips of wood; one is fixed to a board, the second is tacked down each time it is needed to hold the dowel in position (*below*). Pilot the holes with a fine bradawl, then use a $\frac{1}{16}$ in (1.5 mm) drill bit in a pin vice, or an electric minidrill to drill in $\frac{1}{16}$ in (1.5 mm).

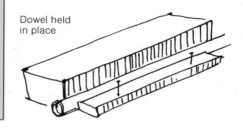

Dowel held
in place

Cut four slats for the back $1\frac{1}{16}$ in (27 mm) long, from $\frac{1}{16} \times \frac{3}{16}$ in (1.5 × 5 mm) wood, shape the top bar from a $\frac{1}{16} \times \frac{3}{8}$ in (1.5 × 9 mm) strip – you can pare it with a craft knife, or use a fretsaw (see page 71). For the seat frame and stretchers, cut eight lengths of $\frac{1}{16}$ in (1.5 mm) dowel $1\frac{1}{8}$ in (29 mm) long, and two $1\frac{5}{8}$ in (42 mm) long to fit between the front legs, which are wider apart.

Check that the two bars fit into the holes in the back legs, and the slats, which are to be butt-joined, will fit between the uprights. Draw parallel guide lines on a thin strip of card or wood $\frac{1}{16}$ in (1.5 mm) thick by $\frac{7}{8}$ in (22 mm) wide by 4 in (100 mm) long, marking the top of the seat $1\frac{1}{2}$ in (38 mm) up, and allowing $\frac{1}{4}$ in (6 mm) gaps between the slats. Laid between the two uprights, this will act as a spacer as well as a guide for correct positioning of the slats.

Use small dabs of glue to fit the $\frac{1}{16}$ in (1.5 mm) dowel in position, and hold firmly between two blocks of wood as before (*see top page 67*). Glue the ends of the slats, and position over the guide lines, checking that all of the joints are at a right angle.

Join the front legs in the same way, using the $1\frac{5}{8}$ in (42 mm) dowel. When front and back are firm, more holes can be drilled for side stretchers and seat, $\frac{1}{2}$ in (12 mm), $\frac{15}{16}$ in (24 mm) and $1\frac{7}{16}$ in (37 mm) from the ground. Check that the chair stands square once the stretchers are glued, and hold

Fit bars and slats

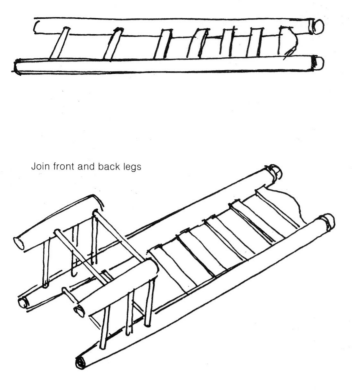

Join front and back legs

MATERIALS & EQUIPMENT

- $\frac{3}{32}$ in (2 mm) sheet obeche or spruce
- $\frac{1}{4}$ in (6 mm) square
- $\frac{1}{16} \times \frac{1}{2}$ in (1.5 × 12 mm) strip
- $\frac{3}{16}$ in (5 mm) square
  $\frac{3}{32} \times \frac{1}{8}$ in (2 × 3 mm) strip
  $\frac{1}{16}$ in (1.5 mm) sheet or ply
- equipment as for ladderback chair

Making the pine table

A simple pine table can be made from obeche, using $\frac{3}{32}$ in (2 mm) sheet for the top, $\frac{1}{4}$ in (6 mm) square for the legs, $\frac{1}{16} \times \frac{1}{2}$ in (1.5 × 12 mm) for the frieze, and $\frac{3}{16}$ in (5 mm) for the stretchers.

Spruce has a distinctive grain, and can be used instead to simulate pitch pine.

The table top is $2\frac{1}{2} \times 5$ in (65 × 127 mm), the legs $2\frac{3}{8}$ in (60 mm), the frieze and stretchers $4\frac{1}{4}$ in (108 mm) and $1\frac{3}{4}$ in (43 mm). Mark out the position of the frieze $\frac{5}{16}$ in (8 mm) from each edge. Glue pairs of legs together, centring the long friezes and stretchers with the stretchers $\frac{5}{16}$ in (8 mm) from the ground. Glue in place outside the guide line, adding the short stretchers and friezes. You can use blocks of polystyrene and elastic bands or masking tape to keep everything square while setting.

If you want to make a drawer in one end, leave one short frieze unglued. It will be supported on a cross piece, and side runners. Fix a $\frac{3}{32} \times \frac{1}{8}$ in (2 × 3 mm) strip behind, and flush with the base of, the drawer. If you can cut $\frac{3}{16}$ in (5 mm) to an L-shape, run two $1\frac{1}{4}$ in (32 mm) strips inside the bottom edge of the side friezes – or add $\frac{3}{32}$ in

together with elastic bands or masking tape until set.

Depending on the depth of the holes you drill, you may have to adjust the lengths of the $\frac{1}{16}$ in (1.5 mm) dowel. The front and back of the seat can be dropped $\frac{1}{16}$ in (1.5 mm), as the joints on the full-size chairs were often staggered to avoid weakening the posts. Always use glue sparingly; if you want to stain the wood you will find the colour will not penetrate any glued areas.

The rush seat can be made of fine twine (hemp), coarse thread, thin strands of raffia, even embroidery cotton. Start with a knotted loop on one side of the frame, take the twine under the opposite side, up and back, under the first strand and parallel frame, back over the frame and twine, then under the opposite side, repeating the movement in decreasing squares (*right*). Always remember to

overlap the earlier strands. As you work round, the strands will form triangular shapes, and you will need to use a darning needle to weave through the centre. Finish underneath with a backstitch and a knot.

Weave seat

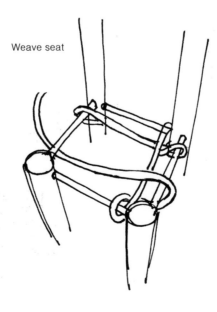

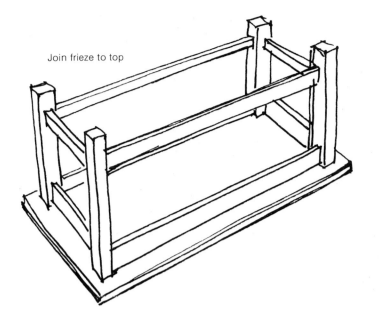

Join frieze to top

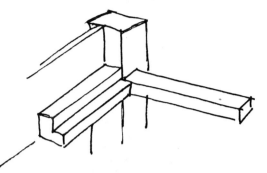

Fit drawer support and runners

Make a drawer

(2 mm) square to two strips of $\frac{3}{8}$ × $\frac{3}{32}$ in (9 × 2 mm) to keep the drawer running straight.

The drawer base is $1\frac{1}{4}$ × $1\frac{5}{8}$ in (32 × 42 mm) of $\frac{1}{16}$ in (1.5 mm) ply or sheet; the sides $\frac{3}{8}$ × $1\frac{1}{4}$ in (9 × 32 mm) and back $1\frac{5}{8}$ × $\frac{5}{16}$ in (42 × 8 mm), cut from $\frac{3}{32}$ in (2 mm) sheet. Turn a drawer knob, or smooth down a piece of dowel, and glue in position.

PINE DRESSER

A dresser is essential for most kitchens, and it makes a very decorative display area for plates, pans, glass and pottery storage jars. The shelves should be grooved to support the plates, and you can even make tiny cup hooks from fine wire. You may have a dresser at home you wish to copy, or see a photograph of the ideal one. The following measurements are taken from the one illustrated on the front cover (*left*), but can easily be adapted to a cupboard, a dresser with open legs with a platform base, or extended to 7 in (175 mm) wide.

Use $\frac{3}{32}$ (2 mm) obeche or spruce throughout, except for the top of the shelves, the top and floor of the base and the drawer fronts, which are cut from $\frac{1}{8}$ in (3 mm) sheet. To make a dresser $6\frac{1}{2}$ in (165 mm) high $\times$ $4\frac{5}{8}$ in (117 mm) wide, cut the back into two pieces $4\frac{7}{16}$ in (113 mm) wide, 4 in (100 mm) high for the top, and $2\frac{3}{8}$ in (60 mm) for the base. To build the bottom section, glue the back between the top, $4\frac{3}{4} \times 1\frac{5}{8}$ in (120 $\times$ 42 mm), and the base, $4\frac{5}{8} \times 1$ in (117 $\times$ 25 mm), and the sides, $2\frac{5}{8} \times 1\frac{9}{16}$ in (67 $\times$ 40 mm).

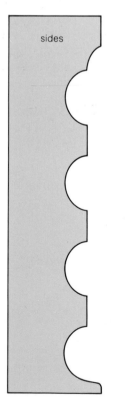

sides

Cutting plan for pine dresser
(actual size)

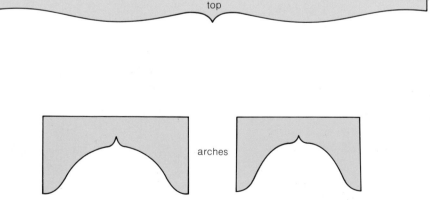

top

arches

Make the drawers $\frac{11}{16}$ in (17 mm) high by $1\frac{1}{2}$ in (38 mm) wide and, for the centre, $1\frac{3}{16}$ (30 mm) wide × $1\frac{3}{8}$ in (35 mm) deep, and use to position the $2\frac{3}{8} \times 1\frac{9}{16}$ in (60 × 40 mm) uprights and the three panels supporting the drawers. Cut decorative arches (*bottom page 70*), and fill in below the base with a strip of $\frac{3}{16}$ in (5 mm). Add drawer knobs.

Score the back of the shelves to resemble planking (the grain must run vertically). The sides are scalloped but can be left straight and are 1 in (25 mm) wide at the top, and $1\frac{1}{8}$ in (29 mm) where they join the base unit. The three shelves are $\frac{3}{4}$ in (18 mm) deep, and the top is 5 in (125 mm) long × $1\frac{3}{16}$ in (30 mm) deep. The decorative panel below and the bevelling are optional. When the shelves are firm join the two units.

REGENCY DINING CHAIR

MATERIALS & EQUIPMENT

- $\frac{1}{8}$ in (3 mm) sheet mahogany or walnut
- French polish
- glasspaper or sandpaper
- wire wool
- fabric for upholstery
- PVA glue
- wadding
- masking tape, elastic bands

Making a Regency chair

A Regency sabre leg chair is quite straightforward to make. You can cut each side in one piece using a fretsaw, but will find it easier and more economical to cut three pieces, making sure the grain runs along the greatest length. This will make the sides much stronger, as the straight grain could

split where the seat joins the uprights. You need a sheet of $\frac{1}{8}$ in (3 mm) wood; walnut and mahogany are stronger and will not need staining, while obeche and other light woods will need grain-filling and staining before finishing with French polish, varnish, or simply polishing.

Cut two sides, one back rest and splat (each $1\frac{1}{4} \times \frac{1}{4}$ in (32 × 6mm)), the front and back of the seat if needed, and two arms for the carver version (*right*), using a special extension table clamped to your worktop (*below*). The seat can be cut from any $\frac{1}{8}$ in (3 mm) wood, $1\frac{1}{2}$ in (38mm) tapering to $1\frac{5}{16}$ in (33 mm) wide × $1\frac{1}{4}$ in (32 mm) deep. The back rest must be curved (*right*), so carve away the back corners and the inside centre, and taper the top edge. You may be able to do it by heating and steaming the wood, but hardwoods are generally more rigid than the softwoods.

Glue the three-piece sides together, and tidy up the edges with fine glasspaper. Fine down the back splat with sandpaper, curving it slightly.

The upholstery can wrap around the front and back of the seat. If it is to be drop-in, a $\frac{1}{8} \times \frac{1}{16}$ in (3 × 1.5 mm) strip back and front will be needed.

Remember to cut the whole set of

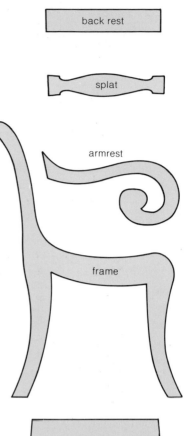

Cutting plan for chair
(actual size)

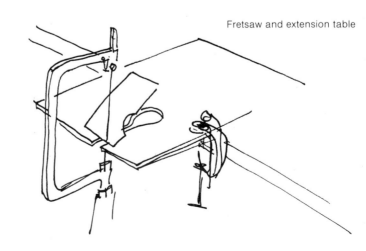

Fretsaw and extension table

chairs to be finished together. Once the wood is prepared and the sides assembled, brush all pieces except the seat with French polish. They can be propped together on a base of double-sided Sellotape while drying.

Rub down with glasspaper (fine abrasive paper), and add another coat. Repeat the process (you will need three coats of French polish) before finally rubbing down with fine wire wool. A final buff with furniture polish will please any houseproud resident of the doll's house.

You can use quilter's wadding, $\frac{1}{8}$ in (3 mm) plastic foam, or thick fluffy lint bandage glued to the seat for padding. Cover with silk, or a thin braid to simulate tapestry. Cotton does not wear well, however, as it seems to hold the dust, but the matt side of raw silk, or rayon with a slight slub, looks good. The suede side of fine leather skiver looks like velvet, and can be cut flush.

To avoid fraying, the material can be cut with a roller-cutter on a self-heal mat, or you can use a very sharp craft or Stanley knife along a metal ruler. The weave or stripes should run from front to back, not across. A fine Regency stripe lining silk or ribbon makes very authentic period upholstery.

The material can be folded round and glued under the seat – allow $\frac{1}{4}$ in (6 mm) each side, and trim the corners to avoid an overlap underneath. Finish with a piece of black paper to simulate horsehair.

Alternatively, a wooden frame can be added front and back, in which case the fabric is glued to the sides of the seat, and trimmed flush with a knife when dry.

Assemble the chair by gluing the sides of the seat, and holding the already French polished or varnished sides in position with elastic bands. Support the seat with a block of wood or polystyrene cut to height.

When the seat is secure, add the front and back frame, if necessary, and the back rest and splat. Hold the back together with elastic bands, or masking tape. Arms are added to the carver when the chair is firm.

PEDESTAL TABLE

MATERIALS & EQUIPMENT
– $\frac{1}{8}$ in (3 mm) sheet mahogany or walnut, or obeche plus wood stain and grain filler
– French polish
– $\frac{5}{8}$ in (16 mm) dowel
– lathe
– fretsaw and extension table
– G-clamp

Making a pedestal table

The top is cut from $\frac{1}{8}$ in (3 mm) sheet walnut or mahogany, or obeche grain-filled and stained. (Note: 'mahogany' wood stain tends to be very pink – a mixture of walnut and mahogany is recommended – so experiment first on scrap wood.)

You can make a round, oval or two-pedestal table, depending on the space available in your doll's house.

The pedestal is turned from $\frac{5}{8}$ in (15 mm) dowel; its actual height is 2 in (50 mm), but cut a longer piece to fit in your lathe, tighten the chuck at the end to be trimmed off, and fit the point into the bottom of the pedestal – this makes a neat finish. Follow the design (*above*), or make your own from studying full-size furniture. Remember the bottom section must be straight for $\frac{1}{2}$ in (12 mm), to fit the depth of the legs. Cut a groove as a pilot where you intend to cut the top off the pedestal.

Experiment with different shaped

Pedestal (actual size)

cutting tools (*below*). You can make a curve by holding your chisel at an angle, and old chisels can be honed down to make various cutters. For more details on turning, read David Regester's *Woodturning: Step-by-Step* (see Publications).

Cut three legs along the grain of the wood, to avoid their splitting, and cut $\frac{1}{16}$ in (1.5 mm) slots in the pedestal to fit.

To make a table top 4 in (100 mm) wide, you will probably have to join two sheets of wood. If the grain is interesting, the join can be down the centre, otherwise it is easier to join to one side. Butt up the two sheets and draw the shape, and cut before gluing,

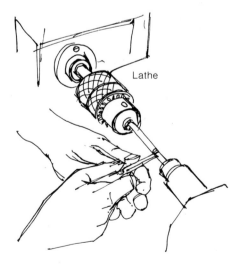

Lathe

Table tops (actual size)

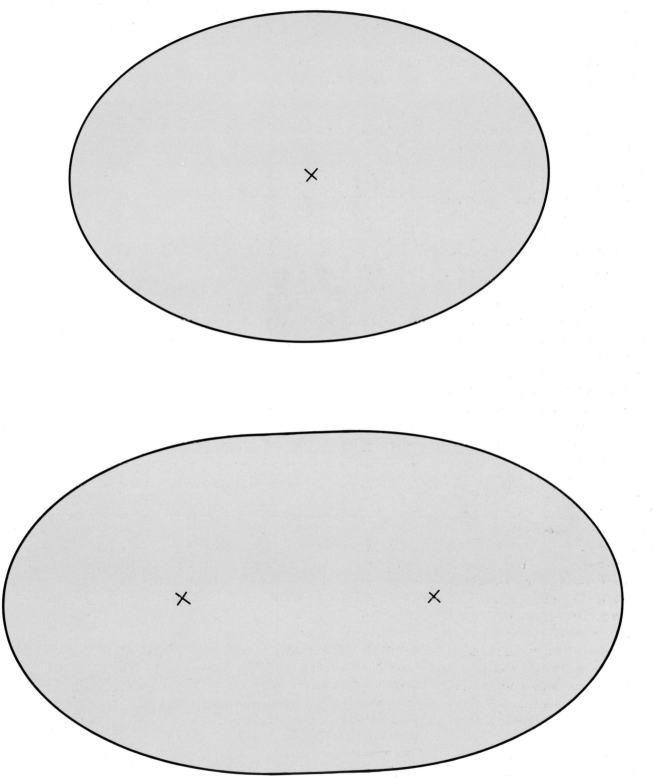

to avoid straining the joint. Glue with white wood glue, tape across the joint and weight with a book.

If you wish to use fine veneer, matching the grain to the centre, and inlaying the edge, you can use $\frac{1}{8}$ in (3 mm) or thinner perspex, which will not warp, and will be completely hidden by the edge veneer. Thin metal sheet is often used to prevent piano lids from warping.

The solid wood table edge can be bevelled – you can make a gadget from a shaped piece of hacksaw blade set between two blocks of wood (*right*), and run it round the edge of the table.

Mark the position for the pedestal(s) (page 73). Make sure one foot points to one end, otherwise the feet will look untidy, and glue. Check that the table top is level.

You can add battens of $\frac{1}{16}$ in $\times$ $\frac{3}{8}$ in (1.5 mm $\times$ 9 mm) to prevent warping. Glue two strips approximately 2 in (50 mm) long to the underside of the table across the grain.

Bevelling tool

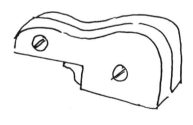

PAINTED FURNITURE

Mass-produced furniture, such as the
nest of tables on page 65, can be
greatly improved by painting if you
choose a style to suit the decoration.
Prepare the surface well by rubbing
down the varnish with sandpaper and
wire wool before priming. Use acrylic
paints unless you want a high gloss
finish, for which you can use a spray
can of enamel over a very smooth base
coat. Smooth out blemishes with fine
glass paper and wire wool. Traditional
lacquerwork has the pattern built up in
gesso, then gilded like the box mirror.
The grandfather clock has been
decorated with paint and découpage
(printed paper) flowers. (See
photograph on page 65.)

SCRAP SCREEN

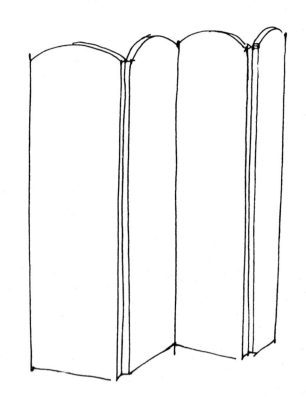

MATERIALS & EQUIPMENT

- old magazine pictures
- scissors
- $\frac{3}{32}$ (2 mm) card, plywood or
  sheet wood
- acrylic primer
- PVA glue or Spraymount
- black cloth, paper or ribbon
- copal varnish or light brown
  shoe polish

Making the scrap screen

You can make a Victorian scrap screen
by collecting pictures cut from
magazines – flowers, paintings,
portraits etc. They need to be printed
on good quality paper, as the thinner
paper tends to turn transparent when
glued and varnished, and the type on
the reverse shows through.

Cut four panels 5 in (125 mm) ×
$1\frac{1}{4}$ in (32 mm) of $\frac{3}{32}$ (2 mm) card, ply
or sheet wood, and curve the tops
slightly. If using wood, seal it first by
painting both sides with acrylic primer
before gluing the scraps (use
Spraymount, Pritt Stick or a thin coat
of PVA on the back), overlapping and
then trimming to fit the panels. You
can save time by using a sheet of
ready-printed scraps shown in the
nursery on page 29.

Join the panels with a sheet of black
paper, black cloth (stronger) or strips
of ribbon pasted down the back.
Decide first which way the screen will
fold and allow enough 'hinge' to go
round two thicknesses on the inward
fold (*above*). If you do not want to
close the screen, PVA glue applied to
the fabric dries hard and keeps the
panels in the correct position; for soft
hinges, apply glue to the panels only.

Finish with a thin coat of copal
varnish, or one with a little colour in it,
to 'age' the paper. A light brown shoe
or furniture polish will give a softer
sheen.

PICTURES

Making pictures

Victorian glass photographs, small
portraits in metal surrounds, fit well
into an antique doll's house, if you
remove the heavy outer frame.
Cigarette cards can make excellent
prints – there are Rowlandson
engravings, prints of colleges, and
many others. Original Baxter prints are
ideal, but expensive.

Small pictures can be cut out of
advertisements and catalogues, and
even a postcard may fit if you trim it or
the room is large enough. Remember
that a picture must not be over 'life-
size' – a portrait head must not be
larger than the head of one of the
inhabitants, the fruit and flowers not
too enormous, although some Dutch
tulips do seem a little over-size. Even
stamps can be used; some of the
Continental ones feature classical
prints, and you only have to colour in
the price.

If you paint your own pictures, you
can start with little sepia 'engravings' –
Rembrandt sketches of people or
landscapes – using a mapping pen and
brown ink.

When copying an oil painting you
do need to use opaque paint, as you
can never achieve the same result with
watercolour washes. Acrylic paint or
gouache are ideal, and can be painted
on smooth watercolour board. A small
piece of Formica with a coating of
primer makes a very firm base for oils,
remember to cut it square and to the
right size before embarking on the
picture.

My own preference is for 17th and
18th century paintings – like so many
collectors I like to create a miniature of
something I cannot afford in full size.
You can paint your own family
portraits, modern landscapes, or
whatever appeals to you. I try to avoid
copies of any very well-known
paintings – after all, a modest house is
unlikely to have the original *Mona Lisa*
or *The Laughing Cavalier* hanging on
its walls.

Another alternative is to photograph
pictures – one friend photographed
her husband's collection of paintings
and framed them. If you do want to
photograph a picture, work out what
size you need it in the final print, and
frame it in the camera accordingly –
close-up, or taking up only 2 in
(50 mm) in the centre. Avoid using
flash, or try a separate attachment
which can be pointed away from the
picture. If you take several shots, with
the flash in different positions, you
should have one print without flare!

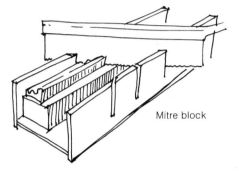

Mitre block

Miniature mouldings can be cut to
size for picture frames, using a fine
razor saw in a mitre block. You may
have to raise the moulding with a
block of wood for cutting (*above*).

If you can only find flat-backed
moulding, without a recess to fit the
'canvas' you must fit a small strip to the
side of the picture, behind the
overlapping moulding (*below*). You
can buy your own cutters for moulding
and picture frames, or make a simple
gadget used for bevelling a table edge
(page 74). You can sometimes find
resin or cast metal frames, though the
metal ones are rather heavy and need
to be hung on a strong pin.

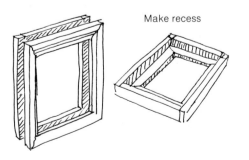

Make recess

From the 18th century frames for oil paintings were usually carved, or moulded in gesso (plaster) and gilded. You may be able to copy such curves (*above*) by adding strips of paper doilies, or gold cake frill, or gold braid, or moulding in Fimo, or even squeezing Polyfilla through an icing nozzle. Unfortunately paintings are usually illustrated without their frames, so you will have to visit art galleries and antique shops to see authentic ones. Experiment with pressing shapes in Plasticine and taking a plaster cast – you can use ball bearings and various sized lids for a round mirror, the end of a square strip for dentil moulding.

One-twelfth scale frames are so much easier to join than full size ones, which can slip apart when you try to pin two angled pieces. Just make sure the opposite sides are equal and the glued joints are square – graph paper makes a good guide. Tape together with masking tape until dry. Paint with Liquid Leaf or suitable gold paint, after priming.

You can line the back with traditional brown gummed paper. If the painting has curled, it must be mounted on another flat card and left under a weight to straighten, as the frame will not be strong enough to keep the shape.

Hanging the picture

Do not forget to add a 'cord' for hanging the picture. Sewing cotton can be attached, one-third down the back, with patches of tape, to small brads (used for electric tape wiring), or to small wire loops. A heavy mirror or a metal frame will need fine fuse wire. Hang on a small moulding pin or a brad, which will only make a small hole in your wallpaper and causes less damage than Blu-Tack or Grip-Wax, both of which can stain and tear the paper. Grip-Wax can be used if you do not want to rearrange the pictures, and is most useful for holding ornaments and china in place, although once it has hardened you will have to ease it apart with a fine blade to avoid breaking any fine porcelain.

PART FIVE

IN THE KITCHEN

POTS AND PANS

- $\frac{1}{2}$ in (12 mm) copper tubing
- small blow torch
- cocoa tin
- solder wire
- flux
- pottery tile
- hammer
- white enamel spray paint
- blue enamel
- paintbrush

Making copper pans

Copper pans are not as difficult to make as you might think. Lengths of copper tubing, and unexpected fittings from a plumbing supplier or ironmonger, can be transformed by soldering a base and adding a handle. You will need a small blow torch, which runs off a disposable cartridge (*below*). A soldering iron does not generate enough heat to keep the metal sheet hot enough to melt the solder.

Cut a $\frac{1}{2}$ in (12 mm) length of $\frac{1}{2}$ in (12 mm) copper tube. File the edges smooth. Make a flat base by cutting open more tube and hammering it flat. The tube will be soldered to this panel (*right*), which will then be cut and filed to fit – a more accurate finish than trying to fit a pre-cut base.

The work surface must be heat-proof – you can use the base of an up-turned pan, or flat pottery tile. Apply flux to the surfaces to be joined using a matchstick or similar wood, or a paintbrush if liquid. This makes the solder flow evenly through the joint.

Solder tube to panel

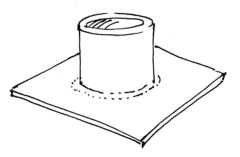

Weight the tube in position, with a metal nut or anything that will not obstruct you, and heat the join with the blow torch. When the flux begins to bubble, the metal will be hot enough to melt the solder. Remove the torch and apply the solder wire to the join, where it will melt and run along the flux, breaking off from the cold wire. Heat the metal and apply more wire, until the whole base is soldered. Leave to cool, or hold with pliers and immerse in a bowl of cold water.

Clip away excess copper on the base, and file the join smooth holding the file at an angle to avoid scratching the sides. The only sign of the solder will be a fine silver line between the two pieces of copper.

The handle can be cut from a spare strip of copper, or a thin tube. A thick strip can be drilled at one end, for hanging, and bent at the other end before soldering; thinner metal will need to be cut wider and turned under by hammering; a tube can just be butt-joined (*right*).

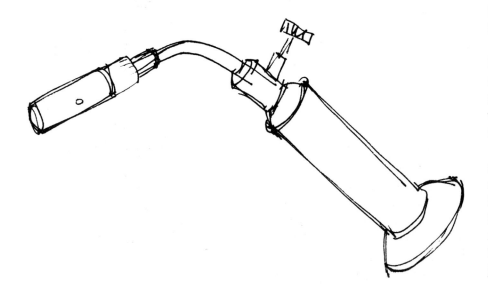

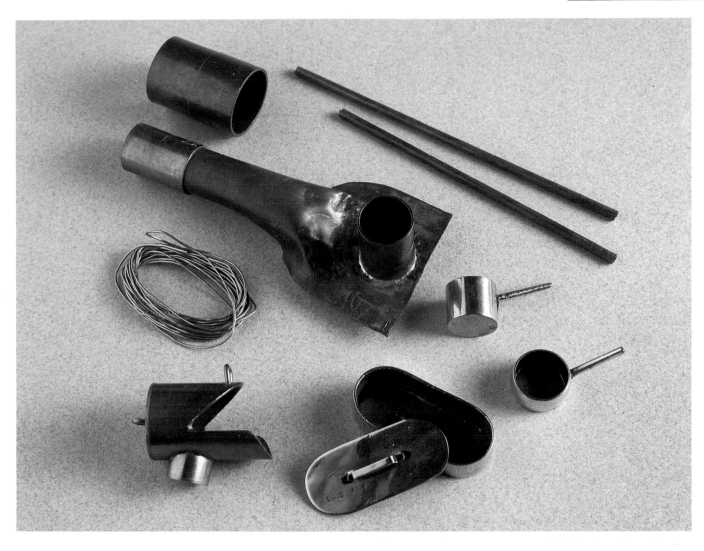

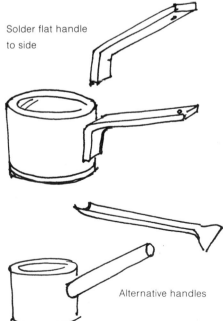

Solder flat handle
to side

Alternative handles

A lid can be made in the same way, cutting a narrow ring from the next size of copper pipe, and soldering it to a flat sheet as before; or from two discs soldered together, one cut to the outside diameter of the pan, the other to fit inside. Make the handle from a thin strip bent to shape and soldered on the top (*right*).

Making other items by soldering

Once you have mastered the technique of soldering you can make many other pieces. You will need to experiment on scrap to start with, and will find that there are only three temperatures – too cold, just right, and too hot. If too

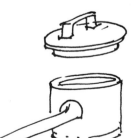

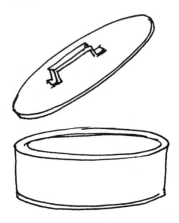

Fish kettle

tabs, to be drilled for the wire handle, or solder wire loops. Spray paint it with white enamel, and paint a blue line top and bottom. If you can drill a hole through $\frac{1}{2}$ in (12 mm) of $\frac{1}{8}$ in (3 mm) dowel, thread the wire through, or curl $\frac{1}{2}$ in (12 mm) wide paper round the centre of the handle until thick enough, as when quilling flowers.

constructed similarly to the bucket. Cut a paper pattern as a guide. You can solder a handle to the top and another to the back, for tilting the scuttle. A hinged handle will have to be riveted with a small copper or steel pin, cut and flattened on the inside.

Silversmithing

If you wish to try silversmithing, there are evening classes and weekend courses, where you can start by making spoons and bowls. In general, try to use the correct materials for any doll's house miniatures, whether making or buying ready-made. Kettles should not be silver, unless they are elegant tea-kettles with a spirit burner, for use in the drawing room. Cast pewter and white metal can be transformed by dipping in Liquid Plate, which adds a coating of silver.

cold, the solder will not melt, just right it will, and too hot it will liquefy and run away.

You can use brass tube and rod in the same way – a fish kettle can be made by hammering a tube into an oval (*above*). You can also cut a bucket from a cocoa tin: work out the shape first with paper, remember it must have a base (*below*), and leave

Coal Scuttle

A coal scuttle can be made by cutting away a part of a $\frac{7}{8}$ in (23 mm) brass or copper tube. The conical base is

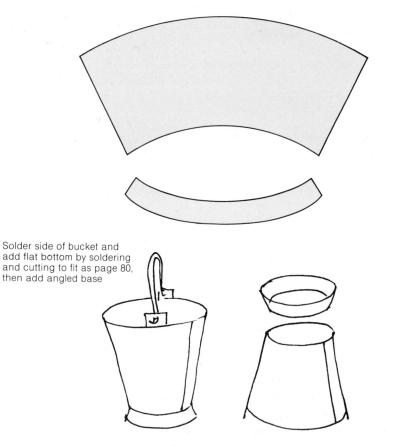

Solder side of bucket and add flat bottom by soldering and cutting to fit as page 80, then add angled base

CHINA

Pressed cardboard plates were used in Victorian doll's houses to hold a variety of plaster or marzipan food. The tea services were of china, fine coloured glass, white metal (softer than pewter), painted turned wood, even the vertebrae of a fish.

Inexpensive small cardboard and pressed aluminium plates are available now, as well as plastic ones, and can be painted with modellers' enamel. A green plastic teaset made in the Far East a few years ago used to make an excellent picnic set – just like the pre-war Bakelite in a wicker hamper.

You can make your own china from the craft modelling clays that can be 'cured' in a domestic oven. If you want to work with clays that need high-temperature firing, small electric kilns can now be run off a normal domestic 13 amp circuit. Terracotta (red clay – for earthenware) needs a lower temperature (740° C) than white earthenware (740 – 770° C), and porcelain (1120 – 1180° C), a green

clay which fires to a clear fine white. You will need to take advice from the suppliers of kilns and clays. Blocks of clay can be bought from artists' suppliers, and must be kept moist.

MATERIALS & EQUIPMENT

- handmodelling clay, for oven- or kiln-firing
- plaster of Paris for moulds
- green soap, or mould release
- smooth plastic or glass worktop
- clay or Plasticine for retaining plaster (can be used with sheets of rigid plastic)
- plastic bowl for mixing plaster
- clay slip, for casting
- sieve (optional)
- knife with snap-off blade
- small kiln run off 13 amp socket
- pottery tiles, kiln cubes
- diamond file
- kiln sand
- glaze
- batt wash (kilnwash)
- porcelain paints, or enamels

Making china by hand

A bowl or cup can be shaped out of a ball of clay, 1 in (25 mm) or $\frac{1}{4}$ in (6 mm) diameter. Make a hole with a cocktail stick and enlarge it (a wooden modelling tool, pointed one end, rounded the other, comes in very handy). Flatten the base by pressing

from inside on to the worktable. Roll out a thin sausage of clay, make a rim for the base of the bowl, or the cup, and add a cup handle. Moisten the surfaces to be joined first, and press together.

You can make a jug (or ewer) to fit the washbowl by adding a rim to a hollowed-out ball, or build up with coils of clay, which are then pinched smooth, applying a curly handle last. Find illustrations of the shape you want – some have pointed spouts, like milk jugs, but most have wide flat spouts, to pour the water into the bowl more evenly (*above*).

If you can master a potter's wheel, you can turn vases, plates, tea pots etc. You could use any turntable – an old

record player or even an icing table spun by hand (you only need one hand to hold a small implement to shape the clay).

Using plaster moulds

If you want to make a number of the same piece, you can make a plaster mould and either press in solid clay, or use it for slip moulding. Slip is clay in solution, the consistency of batter mix, which is poured into a mould. It is left for a short time while some of the water soaks into the plaster, leaving a layer of clay; the remaining liquid is then poured back.

Moulding plaster (plaster of Paris) will not stick to wet clay or a smooth surface such as plastic, glass or enamel. Anything else must be coated in several layers of 'mould release' – soft soap painted on in several thin layers until there is a sheen, like thin varnish.

You can mould your original in Fimo, or look for domestic items to use: a medium size medicine bottle top with corrugated sides will make a pattern for a shallow flan dish, the top from a nail varnish bottle, or a thimble, will make a vase or a flower pot, the back of a button, with the holes filled in, can look like a plate. Do remember that the finished pot can shrink to two thirds of its original size in firing, and the higher the temperature, the greater the shrinkage.

Fix your original to a smooth slab of formica, or a sheet of glass, with a dab of clay. Build up retaining walls of clay or plastic sheet supported and sealed with clay, at least $\frac{1}{2}$ in (12 mm) away, and rising 1 in (25 mm) above (*see top*). Mix the plaster of Paris in a plastic container. *Always* add plaster to water, sprinkling a little at a time until the central mound rises above the water. Leave to 'slake' or soak for a few minutes before stirring thoroughly

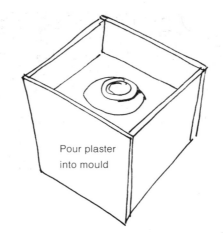

Pour plaster into mould

until the mixture begins to thicken, then pour steadily into the mould. You can tap the table to release bubbles while you continue pouring, until $\frac{1}{2}$ in (12 mm) above the object. Some intricate moulds can be helped with brush work – brush plaster into the crevices before pouring, or work blind through the creamy mixture before it sets.

While the plaster is setting, the chemical reaction makes it quite warm to touch. An hour after cooling down, the mould will be hard enough to remove. Any air holes can now be filled with soft plaster. Leave for 24 hours before using.

Be careful not to pour any plaster down the drain – it will block it. Any residue in the plastic bowl should be chipped off when hard, or if rinsed off while wet can be poured on to the garden as a fertilizer.

Plaster and clay dust can be harmful, so if working often in this medium, wear a mask, and fit an extractor fan to suck the dust away from the work area.

Before casting, brush the inside of the mould with a soft paint brush to remove any dust or loose plaster.

Stir the slip well, so that it is the same consistency throughout – like batter mix or double cream. You can now store it in several small airtight containers, to avoid having to mix the whole jar each time you use a small quantity.

Pour enough for one casting session into a plastic jug, (through a sieve if you wish, though this should not be necessary if it is well mixed), and leave for the air bubbles (like little black dots) to rise.

Pour the slip into your mould, overflowing a little. Small doll's house pieces need only about 30 seconds to collect a thick enough deposit of slip before the rest of the liquid is poured back; if the layer looks too thin, just fill with slip again and repeat the process.

When the clay is firm, you must trim it flat in the mould. Test first – if the clay sticks to the knife, it is not set, but if it is too dry, the moulding may pull out of shape or break !

Place a sharp flat blade horizontally across the widest part of the mould and cut briskly to one side; return to the centre and trim the other side, taking care not to cut into the plaster mould. You can use a craft knife with an extending snap-off blade (*below*).

When the casting shrinks away from the mould, it can be tipped out. It is in the 'leather' state and easily distorted, but may be cleaned or smoothed gently with a damp sponge. It should be bone dry in two hours, and ready for firing.

This unfired clay, known as 'greenware', is very fragile. If you have to transfer it to a kiln elsewhere, pack it very carefully – posting is not recommended.

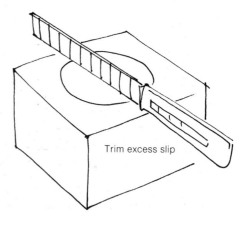

Trim excess slip

Firing

Pottery tiles can be used as stacking shelves, matt side up, supported on kiln cubes to the correct height. A fine coating of special sand on each surface allows the greenware to shrink without stress – as if sitting on ball bearings.

Follow the manufacturer's instructions. Porcelain will take 6 to 8 hours for the kiln to build up to the high temperature needed. It will take an equal time to cool down, preferably overnight before the bisque pieces can be removed.

Any minor blemishes can be removed with a diamond file – unlike sandpaper or a metal file, this leaves no contaminating deposit. Use this to also remove excess glaze from the base or foot after the second firing.

Decoration

The blanks can now be decorated with underglaze paints – the only problem is that they fire to a quite different colour, so you can not judge the final effect while painting. It is easier to glaze first, apply porcelain paints or transfers, and fire again, at a much lower temperature. Some artists use enamels over the glaze, or paint very fine designs on the bisque (unglazed) ware with acrylic paints, protected by varnish.

Apply the glaze by dipping or painting. When the glaze is touch-dry, clean any glaze off the base with a damp cloth (a felt buffer from a mini-drill comes in very useful). On no account must glaze touch the floor or shelves of the kiln – the piece will be welded in position.

Use batt wash, or kiln wash, which dries to a soft powdery finish, to prevent any glaze adhering to the shelves or base. Only coat the top surfaces of the shelves, and always use them that way up, to avoid any batt wash flaking on to the china below and ruining the glaze. Batt wash, like porcelain, contains kaolin, and must be treated with care. Avoid inhaling any dust.

You will soon find you want to cast more ambitious shapes, which will need a two-piece mould. This is described in the doll making section on pages 94 and 95.

Cold cure silicone rubber casting

Another method of making a mould is cold cure silicone rubber casting. A catalyst mixed into liquid rubber causes it to set hard at room temperature. Once again, build retaining walls, of card/plastic or wood, sealed with Plasticine around the original, which must be protected by a thin coating of petroleum jelly (Vaseline). If the retaining walls are sloped inwards at the top, the rubber mould will be much easier to remove. It should be left to harden for 48 to 72 hours before use. The advantage of a rubber mould is that you can cast some undercuts, as the mould is flexible. It will take plaster, resin (with the addition of ground marble this makes excellent fireplaces), even molten white metal which can be heated in a ladle over the stove.

The small bust of Queen Victoria in the dining-room on page 89 was cast in a two-piece mould; the slight risk of an air bubble collecting under her nose was eliminated by brushing through the liquid plaster before it set. To avoid distortion when casting, the moulds should be kept rigid in their original mould boxes. A skin mould (a thin layer of rubber which is pulled inside out) needs a plaster casing. Always take care to follow the manufacturer's instructions.

A word of warning!

It is illegal to re-cast from other craftsmen's designs, or from current manufacturers. Only items out of copyright, over fifty years old may be copied. Too many unscrupulous people have tried to cash in on other craftsmen's work.

PART SIX

THE HOUSEHOLD

DOLLS

Traditional dolls

The earliest doll's house dolls, dating from the seventeenth century, were made of wood, turned and painted, and the more elegant ones had wax heads and limbs, with fabric bodies. Ceramic, or ceramic and cloth, dolls were available from the mid-19th century.

You can still find Victorian doll's house dolls, in scales varying from 1 in = 1 ft (1:12), down to $\frac{1}{2}$ in = 1 ft (1:24). Some even have inset blown glass eyes, just like the larger dolls, and hair fixed through a hole in the top of the head. Many of the current commercial moulds are cast from the simpler Victorian dolls with moulded hair. You can buy moulds to cast and fire your own dolls, or kits to make up and dress yourself.

A shoulder-head can be glued to the body; if holes are drilled in the corners of the 'greenware' at the leather stage, it can be stitched in place (*left*). Traditionally the bodies were made of fine cotton fabric stuffed with sawdust. The limbs were cotton tubes fitted to the top of the arm and the leg with a dab of glue, secured with a twist of sewing cotton bound round to catch in a groove before turning right side out.

These dolls had straight legs, and would not sit neatly in chairs. Instead of enclosing pipecleaners in the cotton to overcome this, doll makers now tend to build up the bodies and limbs with wadding round the pipe cleaners. Each doll's figure can be modelled individually, to be a short plump cook, or a tall broad-shouldered man, etc.

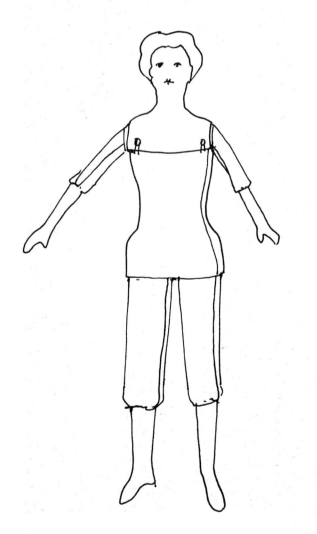

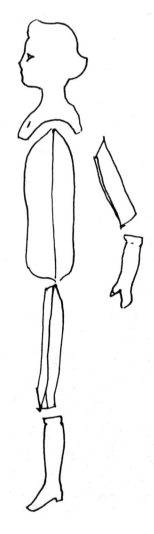

MATERIALS & EQUIPMENT

– porcelain components
– wadding
– glue
– sewing cotton
– pipecleaners
– mohair or viscose hair
– modelling clays, for oven or kiln
– casting and firing materials as
  for China

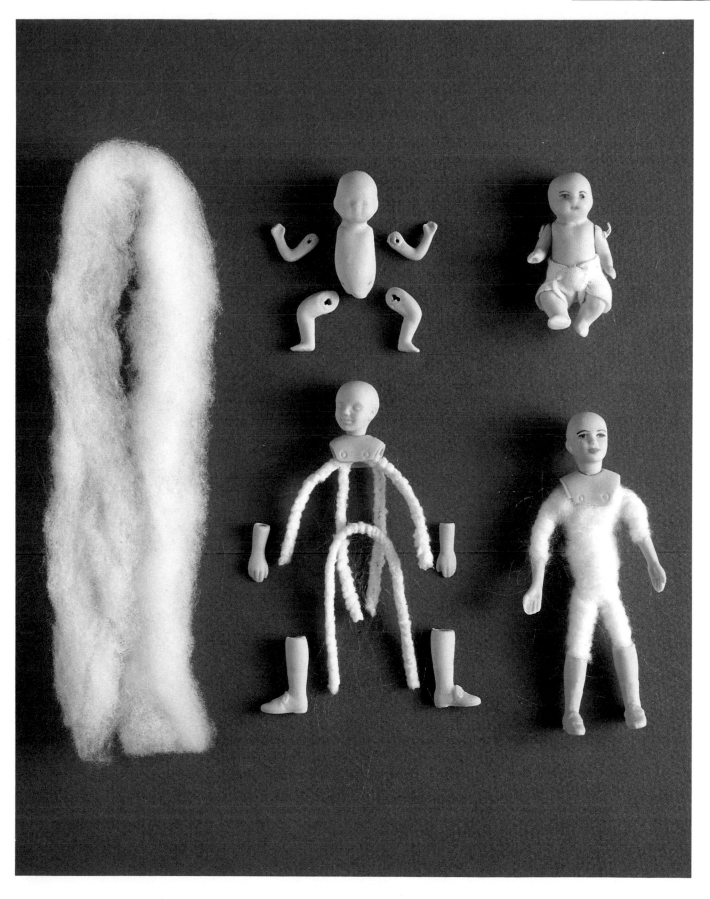

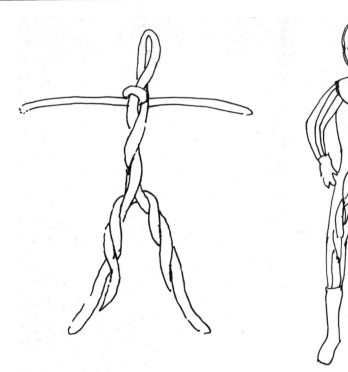

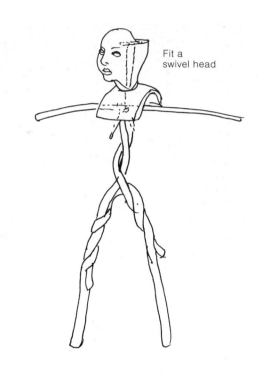

Fit head
and limbs

Fit a
swivel head

Making a doll

To make up one doll you need three 6 in (150 mm) pipecleaners, a hollow head, legs and arms (to fit the pipecleaners), and wadding and glue (clear Bostik or similar). Bend one pipecleaner in half, then twist one-third down to fit the neck (*top left*). Twist the bottom third of the wire and join to the second folded pipecleaner, which will form the legs. The third pipecleaner is doubled round each side of the loop below the neck, to make the arms.

Draw the proportions of the doll, and fit the porcelain pieces on to the pipecleaner skeleton, cutting short where necessary. Allow for the shoulder width. Elbows are at waist level, wrists should align with the top of the legs, and hands finish level with the bottom. Remove the porcelain and bind the pipecleaners with wadding, starting with the chest, to build up a realistic body and limbs. Wind cotton thread round the wadding to keep in position. Glue the head, hands and

feet (*above*). When you come to dress the doll, you can add more wadding if you wish to make her plumper.

The girl shown can be cast from a commercial set of three moulds. Pour the slip without interruption to prevent join lines in the casting. Have a thin stick of cane or similar wood to hand to agitate the slip, to eliminate air bubbles.

When pouring the head be careful to leave space to insert a pipecleaner. Trim the excess slip off the moulds, otherwise you will have trouble removing the greenware. You may have trouble casting hollow hands and feet, as the funnels are very narrow and may need to be enlarged.

While the castings are still in the leather state, trim the pouring funnels off the head and limbs and cut the sides and base off the shoulder plate and drill a hole in the socket for a pipecleaner. If you do not want a swivel head, join the head and socket

with a coating of slip and paint over the join with more slip.

If the head is to swivel, cut away a section of the head for access; you can glue in a bar after firing, for attaching to elastic or a pipecleaner, or hold the head in place by doubling over the end of a pipecleaner which is attached

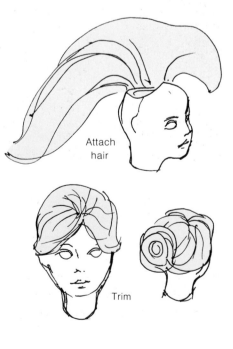

Attach
hair

Trim

though the shoulders to the shoulder wire. When adding the hair, wind sewing cotton round the end and tuck into the hole and glue (*see left*), drawing some forward to frame the face. If the head needs building up, fill in with Fimo, then arrange the hairstyle.

Making a baby doll

The baby shown in the knitwear section is more difficult to cast. You may need to enlarge the pouring hole and use a plastic syringe to force the slip into the head and body cavity without pausing, otherwise the final

outcome will look like a wrinkled Chinese dog! Note that the arms and legs are part of the same mould, so you must remember how much slip should be filling each hole, and avoid air blocks. Remember to drill holes in limbs for attaching with wire or elastic.

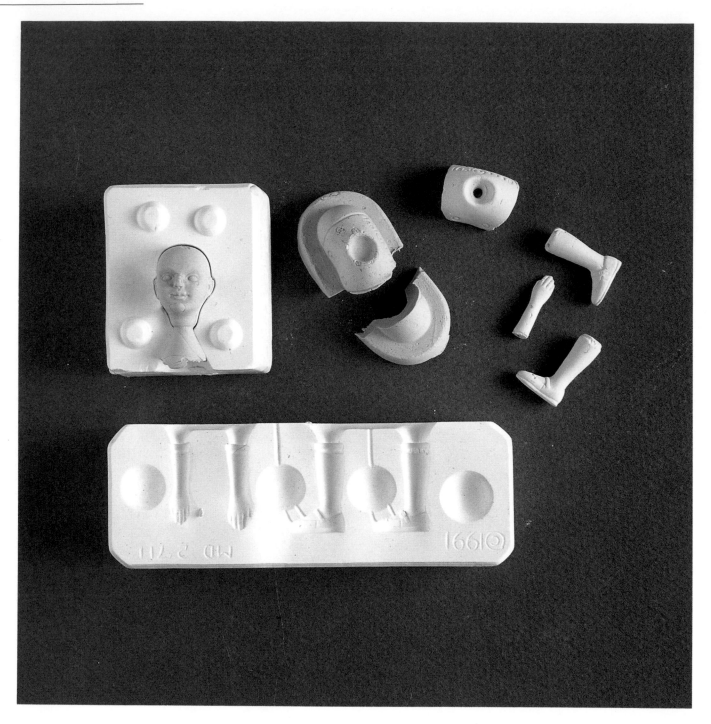

Modelling your own design

You can model your own doll in Fimo (see section on food, page 54), or with very fine clay called Klaycos, which is only available in 8 kilo containers. If you wish to make a mould for porcelain you must remember to increase all measurements by up to 50 per cent, to allow for shrinkage in firing. Before spending time modelling the face, you can check the exact shrinkage by measuring a simple casting, such as a bowl, before and after firing. You may find it helps to sketch out the features the correct size, then scale them up.

You will need to make a two-piece mould. Model solid shoulders, to be cut away in the leather state. Set the head on a $\frac{1}{2}$ in (12 mm) bed of soft clay or plasticine, tilted backwards to avoid an undercut below the chin. Make a watertight box of plastic at least $\frac{1}{2}$ in (12 mm) away from the head, and rising more than $\frac{1}{2}$ in (12 mm) above it. If the base of the shoulders is not flush with the side, you will need to add a block of clay to keep the space open for casting.

Build up the clay to a halfway line on the head. Smooth the surface level and make two indentations with a small marble or round object to key the two moulds.

Coat the plaster and head with a thin layer of mould release, and pour liquid plaster to cover by at least $\frac{1}{2}$ in (12 mm).

When the plaster is hard and has cooled down (about one hour), release the mould from the box. Turn the mould on its back, with the head still in position, and remove the masking of clay or Plasticine. Replace the plastic walls, coat the head and plaster with mould release, and then cast the back of the mould in the same way.

The mould will not be ready for use for another 24 hours. When you come to cast the head, hold the mould together with firm elastic bands. Pour the slip in from the neck as before (page 92), and trim flat before setting. When the greenware is still in the leather state, trim the shoulders, and if wished, drill four holes for sewing the head to the body.

You can use one mould for the arms and legs, and although you can form pouring funnels with clay, it is easier to mould the tops of the limbs flush with the edge of the mould.

All-porcelain dolls (some adults and most babies) will need drilling in the 'leather' hardness state, so that a fine wire can be passed through the shoulders and knotted outside each arm, and through the base to join the legs. You can also use elastic.

Follow the traditional method of painting the features – a dab of colour (blue looks better than brown) for each iris, and a quick brush stroke of brown for the eyebrows and top eyelashes. If you try to indicate the bottom lashes the doll is likely to squint, and in this scale they would be hardly visible. Finally, paint the lips a natural pink.

PETS

Once you have the occupants of the doll's house, they should have some pets. There are now some well-modelled mass-produced dogs and cats available, and more expensive hand painted pewter ones. You might find some bright metal animals in gift shops which can be painted with matt enamel. An inexpensive plastic tortoise can be given a hibernation box (using a matchbox), and painted in more detail.

You can model your own animals in Fimo or similar oven-hardened clays. If working in clay to be kiln-fired, do not let the clay dry out until you have finished modelling, keep it wrapped in damp cloths and plastic, then leave for a day or two to dry out completely before firing. Make a compact shape, keep the tail tucked in and the legs together.

Milliput is a useful material consisting of a stick of resin and a hardener which set rock hard a few hours after being kneaded together, available in white or grey. It does not shrink, so can be modelled over a wire armature, and is ideal for shaping legs and tails. When moistened the finished surface becomes sticky, and fur can be added.

A short haired dog can be coated with finely chopped fibres, unravelled from suitably coloured fabrics, or from skeins of embroidery cotton. Use a craft knife like a parsley chopper. For longer fur use mohair (see the Afghan opposite), or even animal fur – my Shih Tzus produce marvellous wool when combed which I intend to use for doll's hair. The fur will need applying in small tufts working from the legs upwards, laid in the direction the fur grows. Use white PVA glue to fix fur to clay models.

Pipecleaners can also be used to make a realistic dog with a furry coat, and are available in black as well as white, but the finished animal can be painted the correct colour with a thin coat of acrylic or other water-based paint. To stipple or shade one colour into another use almost dry paint on a small toothbrush.

The dog's shape is built up by winding pipecleaners round a basic skeleton of twisted pipecleaners. This material suits the square chunky build of most dogs, whereas cats' heads need to be more sharply defined, and are better modelled in a clay.

Klaycos, mentioned in the previous chapter, is a very fine grain material that air-hardens without heat, and can be sculpted in fine detail. Some clays can be pushed through a wire sieve to make a texture resembling long fur.

Parrots, wild birds, rabbits, anything can be added to the household, and birdcages and even goldfish in a bowl are available.

APPENDICES

CONTRIBUTING CRAFTSMEN

Bed linen

Ann Underwood first sold me a pedlar doll in the mid-seventies, and went on to make bedding, mattresses, mops and brooms, brush and pans, and all sorts of useful kitchen accessories. She opened a craft shop in her village for a few years, but found that running the shop allowed her too little time to make her own miniatures. She has explained how she makes the mattress. The eiderdown is from Audrey Johnson of Quality Dolls House Miniatures.

Quilts

Ursula Simon is a talented quilter who always preferred working on small quilts . She has exhibited small quilts from 12 to 36 in (300 to 900 mm) square. When she discovered my shop, she launched into making doll's house patchworks, usually log cabin, and some from squares and hexagons. She is also an aero biologist, specializing in fungi, and is now busy counting fungus spores to monitor their effect on asthma sufferers. She no longer has time for needlework, so I am particularly grateful to her for making up all the in-between stages to explain how her patchwork is made.

Table linen

Lynne Johnson has always had an interest in craft work, and likes to excel in anything she makes. She worked in an office until made redundant in 1983, and having heard something of the world of miniatures, decided to revive the tatting skills learnt from an old lady seven years before, to make miniature table mats and cloths. With experience she has perfected the art, and would be happy to tat all day long.

Cushions and loose covers

The sofa and chair are from a kit made by Tetbury miniatures. Cushions are by Zara Webb and others.

Carpets

Anne Pearson designed this rug for me in the 1970s, when she was working on some designs for doll's house needlepoint, and it was sold as a kit for some years. I chose this design out of hundreds, as a typical antique rug I should really like to own. The three colour combinations make it adaptable for any colour scheme.

Anne was an interior decorator, but her interest in needlepoint took over, and she opened a school of needlepoint in London over twenty years ago. She has written five books on the subject, the most recent, *The Complete Needlepoint Course* (Century Hutchinson).

In 1992 she and her husband moved to Norwich, where she continues to teach all levels of needlepoint, and runs weekend courses, as well as selling miniature kits.

The string mat was charted by Donna Brown of Avon Miniatures (see China), who once pulled apart a full-sized mat to see how it worked. I am indebted to her for her detailed description. The larger mat is by Ann Underwood.

Lingerie

Carol Blakemore has been making doll's house lingerie and underwear since 1989. She was a dressmaker, specializing in wedding dresses, and once she started experimenting with miniature clothing found it took up much less space and had a much quicker turnover. Her little corsets, petticoats and negligees have been flung around many doll's house bedrooms, and are available from specialist shops. She has made up a nightdress and negligee especially for the photograph.

Dresses

Jill Bennett trained as a theatrical designer, designing sets as well as costumes. She started making miniature figures, mostly fairy tale and fantasy subjects, while also working as a successful children's book illustrator. When she realized there was a demand for a well-designed range of dolls for the growing number of shops to stock in the late 1970s, she launched her J Designs people, modelling them and making the moulds herself. She now keeps a team of three helpers very busy casting and dressing the dolls, one of which is shown on page 9. For this book she has designed simple dresses to fit two Heritage Dolls, which can also be cast from Seeley Moulds (page 36), and then added the hairstyles.

Hats

Margaret Williams was given a doll's house on her sixtieth birthday, when she retired from being a doctor, and decided to make the furnishings herself. It became a family hobby as her husband, also a doctor, started making and framing pictures for the house. She had a very busy retirement making hats, food and little Fimo slippers to sell at fairs and through shops.

Knitting

June Stowe has been collecting doll's houses for fifteen years, and from 1985 to 1993 she was editor of *International Dolls House News*. This was started by a group of collectors in 1966, the first doll's house magazine in Britain, and combines the interests of collectors of new as well as antique doll's houses. June designed the set of baby clothes for this book; she is a keen knitter, but found the magazine took up too much of her time.

Toys

Angela Potter trained as an architect, but has been fully occupied bringing up four children and running a household. When I first met her she was busy laying York slabs and re-plumbing the house. She has worked in The Dolls House for over ten years, part-time, and has used her practical skills to make small toys and umbrellas, and assemble metal kits of stoves and sewing machines. We planned the toys, nostalgic for our war-time rabbits and favourite teddies, and she worked out the patterns. The cottage doll's house is taken from the design in *Build a Doll's House*.

Books

Elizabeth Falla is a bookbinder who enjoys making miniature books for relaxation, and transforms cheap bibles into leather-bound family bibles in which births, deaths and marriages would have been recorded, on the blank first pages.

Food

Christine Lincoln's food always looks quite delicious. She herself is a good cook, but quite often she and her husband find the cupboard is bare after working on some particularly tasty miniatures! Ray builds butchers' and grocers' shops, and wooden trays to take Christine's food.

She described how she uses Fimo to make her realistic cheeses and cakes, meat and slabs of wet fish, which she has been producing full-time since 1984.

Judith Landry is an enthusiastic collector who discovered she could make certain pieces for herself, and any extras she could sell to support her hobby. She keeps me supplied with crates of fruit and vegetables, licorice allsorts and Kit Kat. Bread dough loaves are from the Miniature Display Company and Lali Shepherd.

Baskets

Christine Baker had enjoyed basket making at school, and went to evening classes to make trays and food baskets. When her children were small and she needed to work from home, in 1981 she started re-seating chairs and making baskets. They became smaller, as she was first asked to make toy dog baskets, and then some for the doll's house market. By 1983 she was working entirely in $\frac{1}{12}$th scale, and two years later her husband David gave up driving buses to work full time making baskets; in 1993 he opened a shop specializing in canework of all sizes.

Flowers

Carolyn Smith discovered paper quilling in 1983 at a craft fair in Essex, and after experimenting found she could make very realistic flowers. For some years she was busy turning out bowls of tightly curled marigolds, daisies, etc. She had to give this up when she started a degree course in 1986, and since qualifying has been teaching handicapped children full time. I am most grateful to her for passing on a few tips on quilling.

Lyn Mitchell, being a keen gardener and artist, started making miniature flowers some years ago for her own doll's house. She works with tissue paper and fine wire. Her window-boxes trail ivy and clouds of morning glory, while her daffodils and roses are finished in exquisite detail. Other plants and flowers come from Dave Becket, Julia Connett, Nadia Whitley, Little Things and Georgina Steeds.

Furniture

Bernardo Traettino was a travel agent in Italy. When he transferred to London he started making simple doll's house furniture and selling it to Heal's. He soon began making furniture for collectors, particularly his rush-seated chairs based on the traditional Continental kitchen chairs, and devoted himself full time to the work in 1976. In 1980 he built a detailed model of Gainsborough's house for me to include in a doll's house exhibition at the artist's birthplace in Sudbury. He now builds very fine houses to commission; an 1860s Georgetown house went to Dallas; a Queen Anne brick house was modelled on its owner's house; a Shaker house is complete with fold-up beds. He has also worked hard to promote the British Toymakers' Guild, established in 1955 to improve the standards and encourage the work of small craftsmen engaged in toymaking. He still finds time to make some furniture, and has explained how he assembled the ladderback chair.

Ian Holoran used to build model railway carriages before he discovered that $\frac{1}{12}$th scale furniture was much more satisfying. For many years, from 1973, he supplied most of my furniture. Some of his finest pieces are on display at Glamis Castle and the World of Miniatures in Oban. He tends to specialize in Charles Rennie Mackintosh furniture, although he still supplies some Georgian pieces to me. The pine dresser was a very popular design that he no longer has time to make.

John Otway was working in the West Indies as a site manager for some years, and being at a loose end when he returned to London in 1981, he started making miniature furniture. A neighbour who built harpsichords supplied him with offcuts of hardwoods and scraps of veneer for his miniature ones. He is a skilled craftsman with a good eye for an accurate shape, and he studies antiques and reference books for his designs. Like all craftsmen, he has worked out his own shortcuts, setting the router upside-down in the workbench, and designing a simple tool for bevelling the edge of a table.

He and his wife moved to the Auvergne in 1993, from where he sends his miniature furniture by post. He supplied the pine table, dining table and chair.

The painted furniture is by Judith Dunger (lacquer mirror), Helen O'Keefe (nest of tables) and Alan Axworthy (clock). The scrap screen was made from a sheet of scraps printed by Silvia Ambrose.

Pictures

Phyllis Dimond is a watercolour artist, who during the war was one of a team of artists commissioned to record London street scenes, in case they were destroyed by bombing. She uses gouache to paint miniature copies of my favourite paintings. The seascape by Hubert Shipp is oil on Formica.

Pans

Paul Brownhill is an experienced metalworker. He worked as a tool-maker since leaving school, until made redundant in 1982, when he found part-time work as a workshop technician in a school. His wife Janet started making miniature food – realistic country fare, game, vegetables, bottled fruit – and needed plates when she exhibited at a doll's house fair in 1983. Paul was soon making plates, pans, pastry tins, jelly moulds, all pressed out of sheet metal using masters he made himself. Since 1987 he and Janet have been working full-time, trying to keep up with demand. He has supplied the sample pans to show how they can be made by soldering the copper.

China

Keith and Donna Brown came to Britain from Canada in 1983. Keith originally came from London, but his family emigrated to Canada when he was eight. Donna had been working as a commercial artist, Keith taught chemistry in a college, and was given one year's leave of absence. They let their house in Canada, and rented a cottage in Somerset. Donna, to keep herself occupied, bought a kiln, and experimented with making miniature pottery, so her skills have been mostly self-taught.

Within the year they found they could make a living with miniatures, so after a brief return to Canada to sell the house and pack up their possessions, they settled permanently in Britain, and have been trading successfully as Avon Miniatures since 1985.

I spent a very informative day watching them cast and fire their miniature china. They cast some plates for me from the bottom of a two-piece mould as examples, they use a two-piece so that the top moulding is as crisp as the underneath. Transfers of small flowers, or Willow pattern are used as decoration. The Crown Derby style pattern was hand-painted by June Astbury. The turned terracotta pots are made by Carol Mann, the slipware teapot and casserole by Duncan White.

Dolls

Teresa Westbrook was looking for a change from industrial catering when she had the chance in 1985 to take over an existing business, making historical models, with a ready-made market in the UK and on the Continent. These porcelain figures, about $5\frac{1}{2}$ in (140 mm) were in great demand, until the orders suddenly dried up.

Having already used Seeley moulds, she bought their doll's house family, persuaded her potter to do slip moulding, and tackled the doll's house market. By keeping her prices competitive, and running the business economically, she has built up Heritage Dolls into a flourishing concern, employing up to twelve people. She still uses some commercial moulds, but is making more of her own, and supplies the dolls dressed, undressed and as kits. Two of her dolls were dressed and hairstyled by Jill Bennett for the Dresses chapter, while June Stowe knitted the baby's clothes.

Other dolls shown in the doll's house are Jill Bennett's J Designs boy, and in the dining room Charlotte Zeepvat's Perfect People little boy, and a mother by Margaret Ward.

Pets

The pets were made as follows: the Afghan by Ray Ward, the Corgi and Shih Tzu by Linda Farquar Lacey, the pipecleaner dog by Joanne Lewis, and the ginger cat by Karl Blindheim.

Doll's house

Trevor and Sue Cook have been building doll's houses since 1983, when they first turned up in Covent Garden with a delightful corner shop. The impressive six-room house illustrated was built by them as one of the projects worked out for *Build a Doll's House,* and they even made the miniature doll's house in the nursery.

PUBLICATIONS & FAIRS

Magazines

International Dolls' House News
Nexus House
Boundary Way
Hemel Hempstead
Hertfordshire HP1 7ST
(Established 1967. Monthly)

Dolls' House World
Ashdown Publications
Avalon Court
Star Road
Partridge Green
West Sussex RH13 8RY
(Established 1989. Monthly.)

Dolls House and Miniature Scene
EMF Publishing
The Old Barn
Ferringham Lane
Ferring
West Sussex BN12 5LL
(Established 1992. Monthly.)

The Miniature Gazette
National Association of Minature
Enthusiasts (N.A.M.E.)
PO Box 69
Carmel
IN 46032
USA
(Established 1974. Quarterly.)

Nutshell News
Kalmbach Publishing Co.
PO Box 1612
Waukeshka
WI 53187
USA
(Established 1970. Monthly.)

Books

Cathy Bryant, *Tatting*, Batsford

John Davenport, *Making Miniature Furniture*, Batsford

David Regester, *Woodturning Step-by-Step*, Batsford

Jessica Ridley, *The Decorated Doll's House*, Macdonald

Jenny Ruby, the *Costumes in Context* series (including the Victorians, the Edwardians and the 1920s), Batsford

You can also find inspiration from books and magazines on both contemporary and old houses, which show authentic interiors and the household items in a particular era.

Fairs

The London Dollshouse Festival
Kensington Town Hall
London W8
May
(all enquiries to:
25 Priory Road
Kew Green
Richmond
Surrey TW9 3DQ)

Miniatura
The National Exhibition Centre
Birmingham
Spring and Autumn
(all enquiries to:
41 Eastbourne Avenue
Hodge Hill
Birmingham B34 6AR)

There are now many other fairs every week and details are listed in the specialist magazines, who also produce their own yearly directories. Enclose a stamped addressed envelope or international reply coupon with any enquiry to ensure a reply.

SUPPLIERS

Specialist shops (UK)

The Dolls House
Market Place
Northleach
Nr Cheltenham
Gloucestershire GL54 3EJ
Tel: 01451 860431

Dorking Dolls' House Gallery
23 West Street
Dorking
Surrey RH4 1BY
Tel: 01306 885785

Goodies
11 East Street
Coggeshall
Essex CO6 1SH
Tel: 01376 562885

Guiscards
The Steading
Rait, by Perth
Perthshire PH2 7RT
Tel: 01821 670392

The Miniature Scene of York
42 Fossgate
York YO1 2TF
Tel: 01904 638265

The Mulberry Bush
9 George Street
Brighton
Sussex BN2 1RH
Tel: 01273 600471

The London Dolls House Company
29 Covent Garden Market
London WC2E 8RE
Tel: 0171 240 8681
(Established 1995)

Specialist shops (USA)

Angela's Miniature World
2237 Ventura Blvd
Camarillo
CA 93010
Tel: (805) 482 2219

Dollhouse Antics
1343 Madison Avenue (at 94th St.)
New York
NY 10128
Tel: (212) 876 2288

It's a Small World
560 Green Bay Road
Winnetka
IL 60093
Tel: (708) 446 8399

Petite Elite Miniature Museum & Shop
Carole and Barry Kay Museum of
Miniatures
5900 Wiltshire Blvd
Los Angeles
CA 90036
Tel: (213) 937 7766

Washington Doll's House & Toy
Museum
Museum Shop
5236 44th Street NW
Washington
DC 20015
Tel: (202) 244 0024

Craft suppliers & equipment

Aral Dollmaking Supplies
The Old Fire Station
Latchingdon Road
Cold Norton
Chelmsford
Essex CM3 6JG
Tel: 01621 828007

Importers of Seeley Doll Kits, and all
their casting materials. Mail order only

Blackwells of Hawkwell
733–5 London Road
Westcliff-on-Sea
Essex
SS0 9ST
Tel: 01702 714070

Wide range of materials and machinery
for the miniature modeller

Borcraft Miniatures
Robin Mills Business Centre
Leeds Road
Greengates
Bradford BD10 9TE
Tel: 01274 622577

Finely detailed architectural mouldings
& picture framing

Creativity Needlecrafts
45 New Oxford Street
London
WC1A 1BH
Tel: 071 240 2945

Embroidery silks and canvas,
patchwork templates

The Dollshouse Draper
PO Box 128
Lightcliffe
Halifax
W. Yorks HX3 8RN
Tel: 01422 201275

Miniature knitting and needlework
materials, wide range of fabrics for
clothing

Falkiner Fine Papers
76 Southampton Row
London WC1B 4AR
Tel 0171 831 1151

Bookbinding materials & tools

W. Hobby Ltd
Knights Hill Square
London SE27 0HH
Tel: 0181 761 4244

Materials & tools for model making

Old Dolls House
19 Batten Road
Downton
Salisbury
Wilts
Tel: 01725 512736

Doll moulds, materials & equipment

Potterycrafts Ltd
Campbell Road
Stoke-on-Trent ST4 4ET
Tel: 01782 745000

Kilns and accessories

Strawberry Fayre
Chagford
Devon TQ13 8EN
Tel: 01647 433250

Fabrics for patchwork. Mail order only

Alec Tiranti Ltd
27 Warren Street
London W1P 5DG
Tel: 0171 636 8565

Comprehensive range of tools,
materials & equipment for modelling,
carving & casting

Craftsmen's Addresses

Avon Miniatures
(Donna & Keith Brown)
The Quarterdeck
20 Brandize Park
Okehampton
Devon EX20 1EQ
Tel: 01837 53237

Wide range of slip cast china

Carol Blakemore
Quarry House
Twitcham
Craven Arms
Shropshire
SY7 0HN
Tel: 01588 660373

Miniature garments, particularly
underwear

C & D Crafts
(Christine & David Baker)
133 Lower Hillmorton Road
Rugby
Warks CV21 3TN

All types of canework, and kit for a
simple basket

Trevor & Sue Cook
252 Eastern Road
Brighton
Sussex
BN2 57A
Tel: 01273 692744 (Trevor)

Attractive architecturally detailed
houses

Tel: 01273 603054 (Sue)
Realistically detailed houses.
Castings of fireplaces and architectural
details

Country Treasures
(Paul & Janet Brownhill)
Rose Cottage
Dapple Heath
Admaston
Rugeley
Staffs WS15 3PG
Tel: 01889 500652

Copper and brass, card & metal plates

Elizabeth Falla
63 Freelands Road
Bromley
Kent BR1 3HZ
Tel: 0181 460 4995

Bookbinding, and bookmaking kits

The Heritage Doll Company
100c New Street
Brightlingsea
Essex CO7 0DJ
Tel: 0585 292168 (mobile)

Dolls, kits, hair and stands

Ian Holoran
31 Turleum Road
Crieff
Perthshire PH7 3QF
Scotland
Tel: 01764 653861

Furniture, particularly Charles Rennie
Mackintosh

J Designs
17 Eden Road
Elmers End
Beckenham
Kent BR3 4AS
Tel: 0181 650 4031

Dolls made from original designs by Jill
Bennett, with porcelain heads, jointed
metal bodies

Jill Bennett
Mendip Lodge
8 Bathwick Hill
Bath BA2 6EW
Tel: 01225 420828

Now creates her own exclusive
individual dolls, all periods

Lynne Johnson
2 Fairfield Close
Staveley
Kendal
Cumbria LA8 9RA
Tel: 01539 821431

Tatted lace & silk items

Lincoln's of Harrogate
(Ray & Christine Lincoln)
12 Studeley Road
Harrogate
N. Yorks HG1 5JU
Tel: 01423 507326

Large range of fine foods & foodshops

Lyn Mitchell
Pikes Barn
Up Lowman Road
Tiverton
Devon EX16 4LU
Tel: 01884 252035

Finely detailed realistic flowers

John Otway
Les Grands Pariaux
03190 Allier
France
Tel: (337) 0068590

Fine furniture, particularly musical
instruments

Anna Pearson
Keswick Mill
Norwich NR4 6TT
Tel: 01603 451941

Needlepoint classes, carpet kits

Ann Underwood
20 Park Lane
Glemsford
Sudbury
Suffolk CO10 7QQ
Tel: 01787 281372

Bedding & household accessories

World of My Own
Ann & Robin Lucas
18 London Road
Farningham
Kent DA4 0JP
Tel: 01322 862680

Dolls, kits, hair & stands

INDEX